Week-by-Week Homework for Building

Reading Comprehension and Fluency

30 Reproducible High-Interest Passages for Kids to Read Aloud at Home—With Companion Activities

By Mary Rose

SCHOLASTIC
PROFESSIONALBOOKS

New York • Toronto • London • Auckland • Sydney
Mexico City • New Delhi • Hong Kong • Buenos Aires

Dedication

To Mrs. Donna Jean Smith, Orange County Public Schools, Florida, mentor and friend

Special thanks to Ann Hoats and Marietta Huckeba of Lake Sybelia Elementary School; Susan Seay; Terry Cooper, Wendy Murray, Joanna Davis-Swing, and Lauren Tarshis of Scholastic Inc.; and Sydney Wright

Credits

"What's a Yankee Doodle?," "Thomas Jefferson and the Big Cheese," "A Star-Spangled Story," "Kids in the Gold Fields," "More Miracles for Helen Keller," "Star Trek!," "Arctic Disaster!," "Zapped!," and "A Crayon Is Born," reprinted by permission from Storyworks magazine.

"The Golden Touch: The Story of Bacchus and King Midas" from Favorite Greek Myths by Mary Pope Osborne. Copyright © 1989 by Mary Pope Osborne. Used by permission of Scholastic Inc.

"The Smuggler: A Folktale from the Middle East" from Wisdom Tales From Around the World retold by Heather Forest. Copyright © 1996 by Heather Forest. Used by permission of August House Publishers, Inc.

"William Tell" from Baldwin's Readers, Third Year. Copyright © 1897 by American Book Company.

"Señor Coyote, the Judge" courtesy of Globe Publishing Company.

"The Hickory Toothpick" from Literature and Writing Workshop: Exploring Tall Tales. Published by Scholastic Professional Books, a division of Scholastic Inc. Copyright © 1993 by Scholastic Inc. Used by permission.

"How Big Is a Foot?" from How Big is a Foot? Copyright ©1962 by Rolf Myller, Used by permission of Atheneum Publishers.

"Ice Can Scream" by Jane Yolen from Once Upon Ice and Other Frozen Poems selected by Jane Yolen. Published by Boyds Mills Press, 1997.

"School Daze Rap" from Lunch Money by Carol Diggory Shields. Copyright © 1995 by Carol Diggory Shields. Used by permission of Dutton Children's Books, an imprint of Penguin Putnam Books for Young Readers, a division of Penguin Putnam, Inc.

"Sick" from Where the Sidewalk Ends by Shel Silverstein. Copyright © 1974 by Evil Eye Music, Inc. Reprinted by permission of HarperCollins Children's Books.

"Antarctic Facts" from 81 Fresh and Fun Critical-Thinking Activities by Laurie Rozakis. Copyright © 1998 by Laurie Rozakis. Used by permission of Scholastic Professional Books.

"Under the Bigtop" by Mary Rose. Adapted from "Prince of Humbugs" from Explore magazine, January 2001.

"Want Fries With That?" originally titled "A Super-Sized Obsession" by Scott Joseph in the Orlando Sentinel, August 24, 2001.

Cover design by Vitomir Zarkovic
Interior design by Sydney Wright

ISBN: 0-439-27164-9

Copyright © 2002 by Mary Rose
All rights reserved. Published by Scholastic Inc.
Printed in the U.S.A.
14 15 16 17 18 19 20 21 22 23 24   40   08

Contents

Introduction

In the fall of 1999, my fourth-grade reading class included 33 struggling readers, just barely at the late third-grade level. I quickly realized that these children lacked many basic reading skills, such as oral fluency, comprehension and retention of content, adequate vocabulary knowledge, and the ability to obtain information from nonfiction texts.

My roomful of relatively poor readers was, of course, a problem, but it was not my only problem. The state of Florida administers a reading test, the Florida Comprehensive Assessment Test (FCAT), to all fourth graders. This performance assessment asks students to write paragraphs and complete multiple choice questions in response to readings. The results of the test determine a "grade" for the entire school, which can affect teacher and principal salaries and may soon determine the retention or promotion of students. Suddenly, the stakes were higher than ever for these students. They needed help and so did I!

I turned to the research and noted that recent studies (Allington and Cunningham) have shown that a lack of oral reading practice is a main cause of reading difficulties for upper elementary students. I know that oral reading is an activity that can help proficient readers practice and develop their reading skills. It became clear that giving my students more time to read aloud would benefit them all. After all, reading out loud is the basis for the more advanced silent reading that students are required to do for most of their lives and on standardized tests. Too often we move students to reading silently too quickly, missing out on the teaching opportunities oral reading provides; see the box on page 6 for details.

The chock-full curriculum often does not afford enough opportunities for oral reading practice. In addition to reading groups, partner reading, and independent reading, students need one-on-one time with an expert reader who can guide their reading development. The logical experts to draw upon for assistance are parents.

Some Shortcomings of Silent Reading

Sustained silent reading is highly effective in developing students' reading ability and increasing their motivation. Kids learn to read by reading. Yet through about sixth grade, it's not without its pitfalls.

* Silent reading allows students to read quickly, causing them to often miss the main idea of the passage.

* Silent reading allows students to skip words they do not know. This is often taught as a good reading strategy, and indeed it is. But it is only a good strategy if the student rereads the sentence and tries to figure out the unknown word through context or syntactic clues. We do not know if children reread for meaning when they read silently.

* Silent reading allows children to mispronounce words, which hampers their comprehension. Students may not recognize words in print that would sound familiar if they were read out loud.

* Silent reading allows children to maintain misconceptions about the printed material, and teachers have no way of knowing that these misconceptions even exist. A student who routinely goes fishing and has seen her father filet a fish many times is still likely to read *filet* incorrectly. This is a familiar word in her oral vocabulary but not in her reading vocabulary. When a teacher hears a child mispronounce a word, it is an opportunity to make the connection between written and oral words.

* Silent reading does not teach children to read with expression, to use voice inflections, or to adjust the rate of reading to reflect the content.

* Silent reading does not encourage children to listen to themselves as they read, which helps them to correct their errors and ensure the reading makes sense.

For many years, my colleagues and I sought to engage parents' help through various projects, assignments, even games. We held conferences, conducted workshops, made phone calls—we tried everything we could think of. The usual outcome was that the parents we needed to see the most did not come; the parents who did come were overwhelmed with too much information and too many ideas at once. The materials we gave them often included an excess of educational jargon. And there was very little follow-up, so all of the efforts gradually lost steam during the course of the school year. We do indeed need the help of parents, but we know that what has not worked in the past is not likely to work now.

This series of homework assignments addresses the need for more oral reading practice and capitalizes on the enthusiasm of parents. Each week, students receive a short passage to read aloud to their parents or caregivers. Then they answer a few comprehension questions. The parents receive an easy tip to help them help their children with reading. Both parent and child then sign the homework page, indicating that they worked together on the assignment.

This easy-to-use homework routine benefits students, parents, and teachers in many ways:

⊚ **Children have ample time to complete the assignment.** Giving students an entire week to turn in the homework removes a great deal of pressure from busy families. Many parents find that they are more likely to help with the work if it can be done at their own convenience.

⊚ **There is no expense involved.** Because the teacher supplies the assignments, parents do not have to buy, organize, or make anything, another benefit for busy households.

⊚ **Parents become aware of their child's reading ability.** Many parents are unaware of the difficulty of their child's reading material and of their child's reading level.

⊚ **Students get credit (but not a grade) for returning the signed homework page and completing any assignment that goes with the work.** This low-pressure evaluation removes the stress of a grade for the student and makes assessing the work easy for you.

⊚ **Students see the assignment as a continuation of the reading work they do in school, not as busy work for homework's sake.** The practice reinforces the teaching you've been doing, and the content is appealing to students and can be used to support social studies and science curriculums.

⊚ **The parent tips are correlated to national reading standards.** This helps parents become aware of the skills being tested on state and national exams and gives them concrete ways to help children improve their reading. It also makes it easy for you to target the specific needs of your students.

⊚ **The assignments are instant homework.** Instead of having to hunt for or create meaningful assignments correlated with your curriculum, you can simply reproduce these standard-based activities.

⊚ **The homework encourages communication between parents and teacher.** Parents receive a letter from you every week, helping them feel connected to what's going on in their child's classroom.

@ **The 30 homework lessons provided in this book support your teaching of reading.** Each passage is accompanied by a teaching tip for parents, so that they will be aware of and reinforce your work in the classroom.

Reading Standards

Student . . .

Determines the main idea (also called subject or topic) of the text

Identifies relevant supporting details

Arranges events in chronological order

Recognizes cause-and-effect relationships

Recognizes the use of compare and contrast

Recognizes similarities and differences in characters, settings, and events in a story

Recognizes differences in fact and opinion

Identifies author's purpose

Understands the characteristics of fiction, drama, poetry, plays, and nonfiction

Recognizes when text is intended to persuade

Recognizes that the time period affects the language, setting, attitudes, values, and events of a story

Compares works of literature to each other

Compares literature to events in their own lives

Uses text features to enhance comprehension

Constructs meaning from complex reading selections

Uses context clues

Makes inferences and draws conclusions from story elements

Recognizes parts of speech

Understands and interprets figurative language

Clarifies understanding by rereading, self-correction, and summarizing

Recognizes and explains the effects of language, such as sensory words, rhymes, and patterns in text

Uses phonics, word structures, context clues, self-questioning, prediction, and visual clues to identify words

Uses appropriate literary terminology, such as theme, simile, alliteration, onomatopoeia, and assonance

The tips and skills from each assignment have been correlated to the standards that are the basis for most reading assessments, letting you select a passage based on content, reading strategy, or standard. The chart on page 8 highlights the standards addressed by the assignments in this book.

How to Use This Book

Teachers everywhere are looking for simple ways to make their teaching lives easier while maintaining high-quality instruction. They want homework that is easily graded, yet meaningful to the child and relevant to the curriculum.

Parents everywhere are appreciative of homework that can be completed amid baseball practice and scout meetings, between visits to the day care center and cooking supper. They want to know that their child is making progress in reading and that the homework is meaningful to their child and relevant to the local curriculum and state tests.

Children everywhere are delighted to have interesting, manageable homework. Most children enjoy homework if it allows them to have the undivided attention of a parent.

The following series of homework assignments satisfies the needs of teachers, parents, and students. Introduce the homework routine to parents with a letter like the one on page 11, and then pick and choose articles from this book that complement the teaching you're doing that week. There is no order in which you should use these lessons, but here are some suggestions for effectively using this book of homework assignments:

Hints for Success

1. Pass out these homework assignments on the same day each week. (Mine go home on Mondays.)

2. Allow until the end of the week to complete the work. (Mine are due any day up to and including Friday.)

3. Insist that both the parent and the child sign at the bottom of the page.

4. Give credit (or partial credit), but not a grade, for completing the homework.

5. Include a question about the passage as part of your weekly spelling test to encourage students to read the passage.

6. Return unsigned papers to the parent for a signature before you can accept them.

7. Telephone parents who are not helping students with the assignment.

8. Make exceptions. (I had one parent who worked nights through the week. I chose to accept her child's homework on Mondays, so that she could help him complete it over the weekend.)

Assessment Made Easy

1. Consider giving credit, partial credit, or no credit for these papers. Skimming the answers will tell you if the child has actually read the story and understood the tip. Indicate this in your grade book with a check, a check minus, or a zero. When the grading period ends, use a homework grade to help you decide the child's letter grade for the period. If you gave eight assignments during the term, a student who returned at least seven completed papers should receive an A; at least six, a B; five, a C; four, a D; and three or fewer, an F.

2. If you need more justification for your grades, note the number of questions following the passage, and score accordingly. Most passages have only four or five questions, thus, correctly completing all would mean an A; missing only one, a B; missing two, a C; missing three, a D; and missing more than three, an F.

3. Offer a second chance. Occasionally you will have a parent who did not understand the passage and was unable to assist the child. Consider a phone call or a note to clarify things and give them a second chance to get it right. The parents will love you for this—and remember, the goal of this project is to help the child to become a better reader. If he totally missed the main message or skills presented in the passage, this means he did not understand it. Give him a second chance to get it correct.

The results of this homework routine have been outstanding. My students have, indeed, returned about 94% of the assignments—*with* a parent's signature! Their reading fluency and comprehension have improved significantly. Exercises related to standardized test preparation were a breeze and the parents were delighted. What more can you ask of a simple homework assignment? I hope these lessons contribute to the success of your reading program.

Special Note: Many of the selections here are drawn from *Storyworks*, a delightful classroom magazine that I use regularly with my students. The articles, poems, and stories they publish meet the interests and needs of my students. Special thanks to the people of *Storyworks* for granting permission to use the passages in this book. I encourage you to check out this wonderful resource for yourself; visit scholastic.com/storyworks or call (800) SCHOLAS(TIC).

Dear Parent,

Reading well is a key to success in school, on state and national tests, and in life in general. I would like to invite you to help me to help your child become a better reader. It's simple. All you have to do is help your child with one short homework assignment each week.

Each Monday, your child will have a short reading homework assignment that asks you to listen to him or her **read out loud** and answer a couple of easy questions. Included in the brief instructions will be a hint, or tip, that you can use to help your child with the assignment.

That's all there is to it!

You will have all week to complete the assignment and your child will get credit for doing the work. Just sign at the bottom indicating that you did, indeed, listen to your child read out loud and help him or her with the questions.

Please contact me if you have any questions concerning this project. The first lesson is attached and is due back by Friday. Thanks for all your assistance in making your child be the very best student he or she can be!

Sincerely,
Your child's teacher

American History

Passages	Skill Focus	Standard
Columbus and the Arawak Indians	● Recognizing print conventions	● Uses text features to enhance comprehension
And You Think Your Mom Is Strict!	● Comparing and contrasting	● Recognizes use of compare and contrast
		● Compares literature to events in own life
		● Organizes information for a variety of purposes
What's a Yankee Doodle?	● Answering literal questions	● Constructs meaning from complex reading selection
Thomas Jefferson and the Big Cheese	● Using context clues— vocabulary	● Uses context clues
A Star-Spangled Story	● Interpreting idioms	● Understands and recognizes idioms and figurative language
		● Recognizes vivid description in nonfiction
Kids in the Gold Fields	● Inferencing	● Makes inferences
		● Identifies relevant supporting details

*A*s students move up through the grades, we shower them with more and more nonfiction. In science, social studies, math, and health, we assign readings from textbooks, magazines, newspapers, the Internet—all nonfiction, with which students in the primary grades have limited experience. Nevertheless, we expect our upper grade students to dive right in, reading up on all sorts of topics and retaining relevant information, often with very little help from us. But reading nonfiction is much different from reading fiction, and our students can benefit from some explicit teaching on how to approach this genre.

The selections in this section are all nonfiction, and the homework gives kids practice in several skills that make reading informational passages easier: recognizing print conventions particular to nonfiction texts, determining unfamiliar word meanings, comparing and contrasting information, and inferring information.

Columbus and the Arawak Indians

Skill focus: Recognizing Print Conventions

This piece introduces the use of headings, boldface, and italics to set off important words and concepts. It also includes pronunciation guides for new and unfamiliar words. These simple text features spotlight important information and make it easy for readers to find the information quickly when they are previewing or reviewing an assignment, conducting research, or answering questions on a test. Students can also use these cues to help monitor their comprehension. Teach them to zoom in on words and phrases set off in boldface or italics and be sure they understand them. Also, show them how headings often capture the main idea of a paragraph or section. I sometimes tell my students that these are "test questions waiting to happen." I'm sure to draw attention to these print features whenever we see them in textbooks, articles, or other materials.

And You Think Your Mom Is Strict!

Skill focus: Comparing and Contrasting

Related Lesson
See similar skills in "Arctic Disaster" on page 75 and "Antarctic Facts" on page 79.

Kids will naturally want to compare their lives with those of the Pilgrim children described in this piece, although their first reaction may be disbelief at the hardships Pilgrims took for granted! To help them develop their comparisons successfully—and practice a skill demanded often by teachers and on tests—encourage students to compare "apples to apples" when thinking about the lifestyle differences between then and now. Saying that the Pilgrim children had to work hard and that we have lots of electronic toys is not an effective comparison because it describes work for the Pilgrim kids and play for contemporary children. Instead, students should choose a topic or category and describe it for both time periods. For instance, a comparison would be: Pilgrim children had only homemade toys and we have electronic toys from the store (comparing the kinds of toys children play with). A contrast would be: The Pilgrim children had to work very hard and we have to do only a few chores to earn our allowance (contrasting the amount of work expected). Students need to make sure that the things being discussed are on the same topic in order to have a real compare-and-contrast discussion.

What's a Yankee Doodle?

✓ **Skill focus:** Answering Literal Questions

The questions for this assignment ask students to find information stated directly in the article. The tip suggests parents encourage their children to read the questions before they read the passage, to help them focus their attention on the information they will be asked about. Reading comprehension questions before reading the passage is a good strategy for literal *and* inferential questions.

Because a reader must simply find information clearly written in the text to answer literal questions, we sometimes assume our students can do this with no trouble. But readers who have had little or no experience answering basic comprehension questions often struggle at first, so it's important to provide them with plenty of practice. Not only will it help them to excel on standardized tests, but it will serve them well when doing research in the content areas.

Thomas Jefferson and the Big Cheese

✓ **Skill focus:** Using Context Clues—Vocabulary

This selection includes several words that are probably new to your students, providing a prime opportunity for them to practice their decoding skills. The parent tip highlights several strategies for determining word meaning:

* Sounding out the word
* Skipping the word and finishing the sentence, then choosing a word that makes sense in place of the blank and rereading the sentence
* Looking at the words just before and after the unknown word for clues to its meaning

Follow-up: An additional strategy is to determine the new word's part of speech from its place in the sentence or from its grapho-phonic features.

For example, in the sentence "Leland and his neighbors hoisted the cheese up onto a sled," the word *hoisted* is probably unfamiliar to many students. But even if they don't know the word, they should be able to tell you that a verb is needed because Leland and his neighbors had to do something to the cheese, and the word ends in *-ed*. Invite students to suggest words; they may try *lifted, pulled, raised, pushed*. They should only select verbs; if they don't, they clearly need more experience identifying parts of speech.

Related Lesson

See additional lessons on using context clues in "Golden Touch" on page 32 and "The Hickory Toothpick" on page 40.

A Star-Spangled Story

✓ **Skill focus:** Interpreting Idioms

This activity may be challenging because even many adults are not clear on what an idiom is. You can make it easier for families by discussing several examples of idioms in class before you send this assignment home. A quick and fun classroom activity is to see if students can add to the following list of idioms:

down the drain   climbing the walls
put your foot down   keep your shirt on

Follow-up: You may want to have students identify some of the descriptive language in the piece: *stormed, gobbled, stinging*. In a discussion about strong, specific vocabulary, you can caution students about using cliches (which are often overused idioms), and point out the value of strong verbs, specific nouns, and vivid adjectives.

Kids in the Gold Fields

✓ **Skill focus:** Inferencing

Inferring information from text is a difficult skill for students, and they consistently score low on the sections of standardized tests that require them to employ this skill. This selection provides a model of successful inferencing (the author infers characteristics of life in the gold fields based on her research) and asks students to find support for the author's inferences.

Follow-up: Use this questioning technique in other stories and articles that you and your students read: Find a broad general statement (or make up your own) and then invite students to skim the article or story to find support for the idea. With lots of practice, kids can learn to do this independently and develop an important reading skill.

Columbus and the Arawak Indians

When Christopher Columbus landed in the islands of the Caribbean, about 40 million people lived in North and South America. But Columbus did not know that he had discovered a new land. Indeed, he thought he had landed in India, so upon seeing the natives, he called them "Indians." Today they are known as Native Americans. One of the many tribes that lived on these islands was the Arawaks.

The Arawaks were quite different from any people that Columbus had ever seen—and indeed, Columbus and his men, arriving on the huge ship wearing their outlandish clothing, were quite unlike anything the Arawak had ever seen. But despite the language barriers, the Arawak and Columbus were able to communicate in a friendly way. Columbus learned that they could take the poison out of a root called *manioc* (MAN-ee-ock). They then ground this up and combined it with other ingredients to make bread. The Arawak also ate fish, sharks, turtles, and yams.

The Arawaks were impressed by Columbus' ships, the *Nina*, the *Pinta* and the *Santa Maria*, on which Columbus sailed. The Arawak had never even envisioned such crafts, but they did have giant canoes that could hold up to 100 people. (There were about 40 people on the *Pinta*.) They made these canoes by chopping down huge trees and then lighting small fires in the logs. After burning out the middle, they used stone tools to scoop out the ashes. They fashioned huge oars from the limbs of the trees. The Arawak were skilled in guiding the canoes and, with many rowers, could get up good speed.

Columbus learned many things about the Arawaks. One thing that surprised him was that, like the Europeans, the Arawaks also played games for fun. The Arawaks played a game called *batey* (bah-TAY), which was a lot like soccer. It was played with rubber balls, with participants kicking the ball across a huge field. Instead of just playing for fun, the Arawaks played batey to settle problems without fighting. The Arawak did not have any metal items such as knives or guns.

As Columbus traveled throughout the Caribbean, he met many other Native American tribes. Some of these he treated with respect and some he took as prisoners to be brought back to Spain. Columbus made four voyages to the New World, but he died without ever knowing that he had found a land previously unknown to the Europeans. He always thought that he was just sailing around islands near what must be China or India. He never set foot on what is now the United States. Columbus was really looking for a route to the east (China) and for gold. What he found were two entirely unknown continents that contained fascinating people who had been living there for thousands of years.

By Mary Rose

Week-by-Week Homework for Building Reading Comprehension and Fluency
Scholastic Professional Books

Dear Parents

Thank you for helping your child read and understand this article about Christopher Columbus and the Arawak Indians. It contains some interesting information about Columbus' encounters with Native Americans and describes their lifestyle.

TIP OF THE WEEK

When authors want to draw attention to a new or important word or concept, they may *italicize* it or put it in **bold** print. Sometimes they may put the pronunciation of a new word in parentheses. Usually, after a new word is introduced this way, the author will provide an explanation of it in the next line or two. Help your child recognize these print conventions and look at the next sentence for clues to the meaning of the new word.

The Questions

1. How many people lived in North and South America when Columbus landed in the Caribbean Islands? _____

2. What do you think might be similar to *manioc* in our culture? (Please use a complete sentence.) _____
_____

3. What do you think a game of *batey* might look like? (Please use complete sentences.)
_____
_____
_____

4. How did the Arawak Indians make a canoe? _____
_____
_____
_____

We have completed this assignment together.

_____   _____
Child's Signature   Parent's Signature

Week-by-Week Homework for Building Reading Comprehension and Fluency
Scholastic Professional Books

And You Think Your Mom Is Strict!

You have probably already read a little about the Pilgrims who came to America in the 1600s and 1700s. Did you ever read much about the Pilgrim children who came over here then? Well, their life was pretty tough. In addition to not having CD players, video games, movies, or any TV, they also had to work—and not just "set the table," either! They had to do real, physical work like chopping wood, cooking and baking, sewing clothes by hand, working in the garden, shoveling out the barns, and taking care of animals. And they had to walk everywhere they went! No car-pool moms then! No cars!

The Pilgrims had very strict beliefs about children and their place in the family. Most of the time they were not allowed to speak unless an adult talked to them first. They were not allowed to be around whenever anyone came to their house for a visit, and if they did make an appearance, it was for a very short time and they had to be very polite. American children often have a private bedroom full of toys. The Pilgrim children didn't really own anything at all. They had very few toys, mostly made from wood or cloth scraps found around the house. They didn't have their own bedrooms, but instead slept in the family gathering room or a loft. If there was a church or town event, children might be allowed to play games or dance, but usually they were expected to work most of the time, just as the adults did.

But mealtime had to be the worst! The Pilgrims did not have things like refrigeration and did not know very much about being sanitary—it's hard to be sanitary when you have to carry every drop of water you use up to the house in a bucket! Pilgrims were especially strict during meals. Children usually had to stand at the table, while the adults sat down to eat. Young people had to eat what was put before them without complaining and without reaching to get it themselves. Quite often, the children didn't even have plates but shared a wooden "trencher" with another family member—and they ate with their hands or a wooden spoon. While they were eating, they often wiped their hands on a napkin—common enough, but these were not ordinary napkins. The napkins were very long rectangles that would be tossed over the shoulder and would hang clear to the floor. When their hands became messy, they simply wiped them on the napkin. And it was only washed about once a year—yuck!

Back then, there were almost no books for children. When they learned to read, it had to be from the Bible or from a book of morals. The Pilgrims could not have imagined letting children read about talking stuffed animals or aliens from another planet.

The next time your mom asks you to clean your room or put away your many possessions, think of this story. Your mom might be strict, but she is nothing like a Pilgrim parent!

By Mary Rose

Week-by-Week Homework for Building Reading Comprehension and Fluency
Scholastic Professional Books

Dear Parents

You can remind your children of this passage every time you ask them to help out with some chores at home or whenever they complain that you won't buy them the newest gadget! Have fun reading this interesting article about the Pilgrims.

TIP OF THE WEEK

Help your child compare and contrast his or her lifestyle with that of the Pilgrims by having him or her circle everything that describes life in the past and underlining everything that describes our lives today. (You can also use colors, if that is easier.) This helps readers organize the text into two distinct areas for comparison—a valuable skill not only for test-taking, but also for clarifying information in nonfiction texts.

The Questions

List four ways you can compare and contrast your life to the lives of Pilgrim children. Be sure that each time you answer, you are comparing the same subject.

1. _____

_____

_____

2. _____

_____

_____

3. _____

_____

_____

4. _____

_____

_____

We have completed this assignment together.

_____   _____
Child's Signature   Parent's Signature

Week-by-Week Homework for Building Reading Comprehension and Fluency
Scholastic Professional Books

What's a Yankee Doodle?

Yankee Doodle went to town,

A-riding on a pony,

Stuck a feather in his cap,

And called it macaroni.

Yankee Doodle, keep it up,

Yankee Doodle dandy.

Mind the music and the step

and with the girls be handy.

Of course you know this famous song. Americans have been singing it for almost 250 years. But where does this song come from? What exactly is a Yankee Doodle? And what's this business about macaroni?

The song was written around 1750 by a British composer—nobody knows his name. But one thing is certain: the composer didn't like Americans very much. Like most British people, he thought that people living across the ocean in the American colonies were a bunch of unsophisticated slobs. The word *Yankee* was a nickname for the colonists. The word *doodle* was another word for fool. Get the picture?

Now for the macaroni part. Back in colonial days, fashionable men in London wore their hair long and tied up in a bun on top of their heads. They called this style the *macaroni* (aren't you dying to try it yourself?). The song jokes that Yankees were so uncool that they thought that wearing a feather in a cap was the same as having a fancy macaroni hairdo. How insulting!

During the Revolutionary War, British soldiers tried to infuriate American colonists by singing "Yankee Doodle." But their joke backfired like a broken cannon. The American soldiers thought the song was so funny they made it *their* song. They sang it when they marched. They sang it after they won battles. They sang it any time they felt like it.

After the Americans won the war, "Yankee Doodle" remained a big hit. It's still popular today. And nobody seems to mind that it started out as a big joke!

By Lauren Tarshis, Editor, *Storyworks*
Reprinted from *Storyworks,* September 1999

Week-by-Week Homework for Building Reading Comprehension and Fluency
Scholastic Professional Books

Dear Parents

You and your child will surely enjoy getting the background scoop on this familiar song. Please sing and discuss the words to "Yankee Doodle" before you read the article. See if your child knows what a "Yankee" is or what it means to "doodle." Does "macaroni" always mean something to eat? Remember to have your child read this passage out loud to you.

TIP OF THE WEEK

One of the hardest things we ask children to do is show they understand a nonfiction text. Knowing what questions will be asked before they begin reading helps children read for a purpose, which focuses their attention on the content. Try reading the comprehension questions below before you read the passage so that your child is alerted to specific things to look for during the reading.

The Questions

1. What is a "macaroni"? _____

_____

2. What was the original meaning of "doodle"? _____

_____

_____

3. Why did the American soldiers sing the song "Yankee Doodle"? _____

_____

_____

4. How do you think the British soldiers felt about the Americans' reaction? Why?

_____

_____

We have completed this assignment together.

_____   _____
Child's Signature   Parent's Signature

21

Thomas Jefferson and the Big Cheese

A True Story From American History

Back in 1801, many Americans just loved President Thomas Jefferson.

And why wouldn't they? Our third President was an American hero. He wrote the Declaration of Independence. He got the French to sell us the Louisiana Territory, which doubled the size of the United States. He was charming and intelligent. And he wasn't bad looking, if you don't mind a man who wears a white wig.

One person who particularly admired President Jefferson was a man named John Leland. He was the minister of a Baptist church in Cheshire, Massachusetts.

One day, Leland told everyone in town that he wanted to send a wonderful gift to President Jefferson. And he said he had the perfect gift idea: cheese. Not just any cheese. The biggest cheese that anyone had ever seen. A truly stupendous cheese. He asked everyone who loved President Jefferson to donate one-day's worth of milk.

The people of Cheshire loved the idea. On the appointed day, they all arrived with pails of milk curds. They mixed up the curds and pressed the cheese in a huge cider press. By the time the cheese was dried, it weighed more than 1,600 pounds. It was more than four feet in diameter and one-foot thick.

Leland and his neighbors hoisted the cheese up onto a sled. They hitched it up to a horse, and off Leland rode to Washington. He made the three-week journey by himself. He must have been quite a sight.

When Leland got to Washington, he borrowed four horses and a wagon and brought his gift straight to the White House.

And how did President Jefferson like the gift?

He was thrilled! He had his servants bring it into the East Wing of the White House. He kept it there for more than a year. People came from far and wide to admire this most unusual gift. A poet even wrote about it:

> "Some said 'twas Jefferson's intent,
>
> to erect it as a monument."

Finally, on July 4, 1802, President Jefferson decided it was time to share. He invited all his friends and fellow politicians to enjoy this most stupendous cheese.

Most people agreed it was very tasty.

By Lauren Tarshis, Editor, *Storyworks*
Reprinted from *Storyworks*, January 1999

Week-by-Week Homework for Building Reading Comprehension and Fluency
Scholastic Professional Books

Dear Parents

Listen to your child read this true story from American history out loud. By having students say the words, we can hear if they are using the skills we are teaching them to figure out unfamiliar words. (See a list of some of the strategies we've been working on in the tip box.)

The Questions

Write a definition of the words below in your own words. Then write a new sentence for each word.

1. donate _____

_____

2. stupendous _____

_____

3. appointed _____

_____

4. diameter _____

_____

5. hoisted _____

_____

We have completed this assignment together.

_____
Child's Signature

_____
Parent's Signature

Week-by-Week Homework for Building Reading Comprehension and Fluency
Scholastic Professional Books

A Star-Spangled Story

The Birth of Our National Anthem

Oh! say, can you see,
by the dawn's early light...

How many times have you sung those words? Have you ever wondered what they mean and where they came from?

The person to thank is a man named Francis Scott Key. He was a lawyer and a poet in the years after the Revolutionary War.

Those were exciting times. America was newly independent from Great Britain. We were looking to expand west, and to spread our wings as a new nation. But in 1812, we hit a big snag. We went to war with Great Britain.

The War of 1812 was a mess, and by 1814, we were losing badly. In August, the British marched into Washington and stormed into the deserted White House, gobbled down a big dinner, and started setting fires. By the time they left, most of the city was in flames, including the White House, the Capitol building, and the Library of Congress.

Meanwhile, Mr. Key was worried about his good friend, Dr. William Beanes. He had been seized by British soldiers and taken prisoner on a British ship. Mr. Key didn't just sit around and wait for news. He went looking for the British fleet. He found them on the Potomac River. Dr. Beanes was there.

Mr. Key convinced the British that his friend had been imprisoned unfairly. They agreed to set him free. But not so fast. The British were about to launch an attack on Baltimore. The two Americans would have to wait on a ship and watch while the British bombed the city.

It was a terrible night. The British fired more than 1,500 bombs, and troops stormed the shore. The sky turned black with smoke. Mr. Key kept his stinging eyes on the enormous American flag hanging over Fort McHenry. As long as that flag was raised, the American troops were surviving.

In the morning, the bombing stopped and the smoke cleared. Our flag was still there! Mr. Key pulled an envelope out of his pocket and jotted down the words that would soon be famous: "Oh! say, can you see, by the dawn's early light . . . "

When he returned to Washington, the words were set to music. Everyone loved the song. And in 1931, "The Star-Spangled Banner" became our national anthem.

By Lauren Tarshis, Editor, *Storyworks*
Reprinted from *Storyworks*, September 2000

Week-by-Week Homework for Building Reading Comprehension and Fluency
Scholastic Professional Books

Dear Parents

I hope you and your child enjoy reading this interesting article about the writing of the "Star-Spangled Banner," our national anthem. Be on the lookout for a couple of idioms and some wonderfully descriptive adjectives. Thanks for having your child read this passage out loud.

The Questions

What do these two idioms mean?

1. "We . . . spread our wings as a new nation" _____

_____

2. " in 1812 we hit a big snag" _____

_____

List three examples of descriptive phrases that helped you understand this story better:

1. _____

_____

2. _____

_____

3. _____

_____

We have completed this assignment together.

_____   _____
Child's Signature   Parent's Signature

Week-by-Week Homework for Building Reading Comprehension and Fluency
Scholastic Professional Books

Kids in the Gold Fields

Close your eyes and imagine you can travel back in time. You're in California in 1850, just after the Gold Rush begins. You're still a child, but your life is completely different.

In the diggings, your family may live in a tent, a rough shelter of pine boughs, or a tiny cabin. Your chores begin early in the morning when you haul water from the river, collect wood for the fire, or feed your family's animals before you watch your younger brothers or sisters. There is no school, but you will work hard all day long. Your parents need all the help you can give them.

You could help your father pan for gold, or, if you're a boy, you may take his rifle and hunt for rabbits, quail, or squirrels. Girls might gather berries or wild edible plants in the forest.

If your mother runs a restaurant out of your family's tent, you may wait on tables or wash dishes. You might sing, dance, or play an instrument to entertain miners—and get paid in gold dust or coins. When the saloons are empty, you can run a wet pin along the cracks in the floorboards to pick up any gold dust spilled by miners the night before.

If you have any free time, you could play games with other kids. Or, if you're adventurous, you might sneak away to a Native American camp. The Pomo and Miwok Indians have lived in this area for generations. Maybe you could learn a few words of their languages, and trade gold dust or coins for deerskin moccasins. You might also learn how these Indians' lives have changed now that miners have taken over the land where the Indians hunt and fish.

Later, you could pay a visit to some miners. Don't be surprised if they fuss over you and tell you stories, make you toys, or teach you to read. Most miners have left their families behind, and they miss their children.

Every once in a while, you might go to a dance nearby. If you're a girl, you'll be very popular. There are very few women in the diggings, so girls of all ages dance. Watch your bare feet around all those heavy boots!

What do you think? Would you enjoy the danger, excitement, hardship, and the adventure of the California Gold Rush?

By Liza Ketchum
Reprinted from *Storyworks*, April/May 1998

Week-by-Week Homework for Building Reading Comprehension and Fluency
Scholastic Professional Books
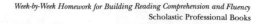

Dear Parents

This week's reading assignment is about children's lives during the California Gold Rush. The next time your child complains about cleaning his room or taking out the garbage, remind him of the hard work kids used to have to do! Please listen to your child read this article out loud and help out with the questions below.

The Questions

1. How was life dangerous? _____
_____
_____
_____

2. How was life exciting? _____
_____
_____
_____

3. How was life hard? _____
_____
_____
_____

We have completed this assignment together.

_____   _____
Child's Signature   Parent's Signature

Week-by-Week Homework for Building Reading Comprehension and Fluency
Scholastic Professional Books

Chapter 2

Fiction

Passage	Skill Focus	Standard
The Golden Touch	✹ Using context clues— vocabulary	✹ Uses context clues
The Smuggler	✹ Identifying when a speaker in the text changes	✹ Uses text features to enhance comprehension
William Tell	✹ Making inferences— character traits	✹ Constructs meaning from complex reading selection ✹ Makes inferences and draws conclusions regarding story elements
Señor Coyote, the Judge	✹ Making inferences—plot	✹ Constructs meaning from complex reading selection ✹ Makes inferences and draws conclusions regarding story elements
The Hickory Toothpick	✹ Using context clues— vocabulary	✹ Uses context clues
How Big Is a Foot?	✹ Understanding story structure	✹ Uses text features to enhance comprehension

*W*hile upper-grade students read their fair share of nonfiction, they are still big fans of fiction. Even though many students are proficient readers and select their own independent reading material, we should continue to teach reading strategies and expose them to new genres.

The folk tales, fables, tall tales, and fairy tales included here are great fun for readers of all ages. Parents and kids will enjoy reading them, and the homework questions reinforce key strategies that help kids to become expert readers.

The Golden Touch

✓ **Skill focus:** Using Context Clues—Vocabulary

Related Lesson

See additional lessons on using context clues in "Thomas Jefferson and the Big Cheese" on page 22 and "The Hickory Toothpick" on page 40.

The ability to decode words by examining their context is an important reading strategy. "The Golden Touch" contains vocabulary that will be new to students, and the homework activity asks them to define the words based on their context. But figuring out a word from its context and using it in simple conversation are two distinctly different skills. We often "know" a word just for the few moments it takes to read and understand a passage. To really know a word is to be able to correctly use it in everyday conversation and in writing. This assignment invites students to create original sentences using the new words to help them add to their working vocabulary.

The Smuggler

✓ **Skill focus:** Identifying When a Speaker in the Text Changes

This ironic folk tale is even more fun when read out loud. Encourage kids to get into the act by trying out different voices for the characters and narrator of the story. Reading in character requires students to note when the speaker changes by keying in to various print conventions and monitoring their comprehension. Remind kids to:

* Look for quotation marks
* Pay attention to new paragraphs, marked by indentation
* Note tag lines, like "said" and "replied"
* Ensure their reading makes sense

You can model this kind of active reading in class—by changing the rate of your speech to reflect the pace of the story, by using expression to convey the character of a speaker, and by inflecting words and sentences so they sound like natural spoken language. The tip encourages parents to read expressively as well. Although reading this way is slower, it greatly increases comprehension.

Follow-up: The focus of this activity is having students pay attention to changes in speakers in a story, but don't miss this opportunity to discuss the surprise ending and the irony of the story. The frustrated inspector tries in vain to find contraband yet misses what is right under his nose. Discussing irony in a short text like "The Smuggler" makes an effective introduction to this sophisticated concept.

William Tell

✓ **Skill focus:** Making Inferences—Character Traits

As more and more states develop performance assessments, students are routinely asked to write paragraphs that describe characters in stories. The exercise accompanying "William Tell" is one way to give students practice in making inferences about characters and supporting them with examples from the text. Doing this exercise with a variety of stories will also help students to appreciate strong characters they encounter during independent reading.

Follow-up: You may want to read *The 500 Hats of Bartholomew Cubbins* by Dr. Seuss as a follow-up to this story. It is also about a ruler who required his subjects to take off their hats and bow to him as he passed. See if students can recognize the parallels in the characters from this book and "William Tell." How would they describe Bartholomew Cubbins? Can they support his description with information from the story?

Señor Coyote, the Judge

✓ **Skill focus:** Making Inferences—Plot

Most children read very literally. The ability to infer information from a story while reading comes only with lots of experience, and "Señor Coyote" is a perfect piece to give students practice with this important skill. Most of the story is straightforward, but there are a few spots where students need to make a mental leap from the words on the page to their implication for the characters: for instance, when the snake offers a "reward" to the rabbit if he'll move the stone, and when the coyote wants to reenact the scene. I have often had kids read the closing sentence—"Señor Rattlesnake was left with lots of time to think about it all"—and not understand the snake's predicament. We need to help budding readers comprehend the import of words—not just their literal meaning.

The Hickory Toothpick

✓ Skill focus: Using Context Clues—Vocabulary

This tall tale is particularly appealing to kids because it is told in the first person. What a wonderful way of making the story seem quite believable—right up until the end! Explain to students that this story is written in dialect, meaning that the words capture how this particular person actually speaks. Students may have trouble at first, but reading aloud and using expression should help them get into the story.

Children who live where it does not snow may have particular difficulty with the idea of a storm actually covering a house "plumb up." And be prepared for the responses from parents who look up "rations" in the dictionary and think that this means that each person only gets a limited amount of supplies for a given time. This is the whole idea of teaching how words differ radically by the context in which they are used.

> **Related Lesson**
>
> See additional lessons on using context clues in "Thomas Jefferson and the Big Cheese" on page 22 and "The Golden Touch" on page 32.

How Big Is a Foot?

✓ Skill focus: Understanding Story Structure

Story structure is a difficult concept to teach in the upper grades because the texts students are reading have increasingly complex structures. It's helpful to begin with a relatively simple structure in a relatively short text—as with this delightful fairy tale. Students can't help but notice the repetition, and hopefully this experience will spur them to look for patterns in words, phrases, events, settings, or characters in other texts.

The Golden Touch

Bacchus, the merry god of the vine, raised his goblet. "King Midas," he said, "because you have been so hospitable to me, ask for anything you wish, and I will grant it to you."

"Ah, well," said the king, chuckling. "Of course, there's only one thing: I wish that everything I touch would turn to gold!"

"My friend, you already have all the gold you could possibly want," said Bacchus, looking disappointed.

"Oh, no! I don't!" said Midas. "One never has enough gold!"

"Well, if that's what you wish for, I suppose I will have to grant it," said Bacchus.

Bacchus soon took his leave. As Midas waved goodbye to him, his hand brushed an oak twig hanging from a tree—and the twig turned to gold!

The king screamed with joy, then shouted, "My wish has come true! Thank you! Thank you!"

The god disappeared down the road.

Midas looked around excitedly. He leaned over and picked a stone up from the ground—and the stone turned into a golden nugget! He kicked the sand—and the sand turned to golden grains!

King Midas threw back his head and shouted, "I'm the richest man in the world!" Then he rushed around his grounds, touching everything. And everything, *everything* turned to gold: ears of corn in his fields, apples plucked from the trees, the pillars of his mansion!

Finally, exhausted but overjoyed, King Midas called for his dinner. His servants placed a huge meal before him. "Oh, I'm so hungry!" he said, as he speared a piece of meat and brought it to his mouth.

But suddenly King Midas realized his wish may not have been as wonderful as he thought, for the moment he bit down on the meat, it too turned to gold.

Midas laughed uneasily, then reached for a piece of bread. But as soon as his hands touched the bread, it also became a hard, golden nugget! Weak with dread, Midas reached for his goblet of water. But, alas! His lips touched only hard, cold metal. The water had also turned to gold.

Covering his head and moaning, King Midas realized his great wish was going to kill him. He would starve to death, or die of thirst!

"Bacchus!" he cried. "I've been a greedy fool! Take away your gift! Help me, Bacchus!"

The sobbing king fell off his chair to his knees. His servants grieved for him, but none dared go near him, for they feared he might accidentally turn them to gold, too.

Bacchus suddenly appeared. Stumbling to his feet, King Midas begged Bacchus to take away the curse of the golden touch.

"You were greedy and foolish, my friend," said Bacchus. "But I will forgive you. Now go wash yourself in the Pactolus River and you'll be cleansed of this desire to have more gold than anyone else!"

King Midas did as Bacchus said. He washed in the river, leaving behind streams of gold in the river's sands. Then he returned home and happily at his dinner.

From *Favorite Greek Myths* by Mary Pope Osborne. Copyright © 1989 by Mary Pope Osborne. Used by permission of Scholastic.

Dear Parents

Your child may have seen or heard references to "King Midas and the Golden Touch" in conversations or on television. This homework is a great opportunity to hear the real story behind those references. Please remember to listen to your child read it out loud, and enjoy this familiar tale, retold by popular children's author Mary Pope Osborne.

TIP OF THE WEEK

To figure out what an unfamiliar word means, try replacing it with another that makes sense in the sentence. For instance: "Bacchus, the merry god of the vine, raised his goblet."

Many students may not know what a goblet is. From the context of the sentence, a reader might try the word "glass," which makes sense. Encourage your child to try this technique for the words in the assignment below.

The Questions

Circle the following words in the story. For each word, think of another that makes sense in the sentence and could have the same meaning; write it below. Then try rereading the sentences, inserting the word you wrote, and see if they still make sense. Now that you know the meaning the words, write your own original sentence for each one.

1. nugget _____

_____

2. exhausted _____

_____

3. speared _____

_____

4. dread _____

_____

We have completed this assignment together.

_____   _____
Child's Signature   Parent's Signature

The Smuggler

A Folk Tale From the Middle East

A clever smuggler led a donkey burdened with bundles of straw to the border between two lands. The inspector at the border eyed the donkey's bundles with suspicion.

"I must search your bundles!" the inspector said. "I think you have hidden valuables that you wish to sell at the market. If so, you must pay me a border fee!"

"Search as you wish," said the man. "If you find something other than straw, I will pay whatever fee you ask."

The inspector pulled apart the straw bundles until there was straw in the air, straw all around. Yet not a valuable thing in the straw was found.

"You are a clever smuggler!" said the inspector. "I am certain that you are hiding something. Yet so carefully have you covered it, I have not discovered it. Go!"

The man crossed the border. The suspicious inspector looked on with a scowl.

The next day, the man came back to the border with a donkey burdened with straw. Once again the inspector pulled apart the bundles. There was straw in the air, straw on the ground, straw, straw, straw all around.

"Not one valuable thing have I found!" the exasperated inspector said. "Go!" The man and the donkey went across the border. "Bah!"

Every day for the next ten years, the man came to the border with a donkey burdened with straw. Each day the inspector searched his bundles, but he found nothing.

Finally, the inspector retired. Even as an old man, he could not stop thinking about that clever smuggler. One day as he walked through the marketplace, still trying to solve the mystery at the border, he muttered, "I am certain that man was smuggling something. Perhaps I should have looked more carefully in the donkey's mouth. Or he could have hidden something between the hairs on the donkey's tail!"

As he mumbled to himself, he noticed a familiar face in the crowd. "You!" he exclaimed. "I know you! You were the man who came to the border every day with a donkey burdened with straw. Come and speak with me!"

When the man walked toward him, the old inspector said, "Admit it! You were smuggling something across the border, weren't you?"

The man nodded and grinned.

"Just as I suspected. You were sneaking something to market! Tell me what it was!"

Donkeys," said the man.

From *Wisdom Tales From Around the World* retold by Heather Forest.
Copyright © 1996 by Heather Forest. Used by permission of August House Publishers, Inc.

Week-by-Week Homework for Building Reading Comprehension and Fluency
Scholastic Professional Books

Dear Parents

As you read this entertaining tale, encourage your child to change his or her voice whenever a new person in the story speaks. You can make this more fun by taking a turn to read and changing your voice to fit the character in the story.

TIP OF THE WEEK

Encourage your child to change his or her voice to express questioning, surprise, or other emotions as he or she reads. It helps your child understand who is talking and follow the events in the story more easily. To help your child tell when a speaker changes, remind him or her to look for the following clues:

* Indentation, signaling a new paragraph
* Quotation marks
* Tag lines, such as the word "said" or "replied"

The Questions

What are three ways you can tell that a new character is going to speak in a story?

1. _____

_____

_____

2. _____

_____

_____

3. _____

_____

_____

We have completed this assignment together.

_____   _____
Child's Signature   Parent's Signature

Week-by-Week Homework for Building Reading Comprehension and Fluency
Scholastic Professional Books

William Tell

Once upon a time a man named Gessler came to Switzerland and took over as the ruler of the Swiss people. He was cruel and treated them as slaves. Among the beautiful mountains of that country, there lived a brave huntsman called William Tell. In all the world there was no one who could shoot with a bow and arrows as well as he. Tell hated the cruel Gessler and the strangers that had come with him into Switzerland.

One day Gessler hung his hat on a tall pole in the town square. Then he gave orders that every man who passed by should bow to this hat. There was one man and one child who would not do this—William Tell and his son.

When Gessler heard that Tell had passed the pole and not bowed to his hat, he was glad because he had now a good excuse for putting Tell in prison. Gessler had long been afraid of the huntsman, and wanted very much to put him where he could do no harm.

William Tell and his son were kept in prison for a long time. Gessler did not mean that they should ever be free again.

One day Gessler thought of a cruel plan. He ordered Tell to be brought before him. "I hear," he said, "that you can shoot well with a bow and arrows."

Tell answered, "That is so."

"Then that is just what I want you to do," said Gessler, "and that is what you shall do. Tomorrow, your son shall stand at one side of the public square, with an apple on his head. You shall stand at the other side and shoot the apple with an arrow."

"You do not mean it," said Tell.

"I do," said Gessler. "If you will not do it, your son shall be killed before your eyes."

"You want me to kill my boy," he said.

"No," said Gessler, "I want you to shoot the apple. If you do not hit it, both you and your boy shall die."

"And what if I do hit it?" asked Tell.

"Then both of you shall go free," said Gessler. And so at last Tell said he would try.

The next day the little boy was made to stand up at one side of the public square with a small apple on his head. "I am not afraid, father," he said. "I know you will hit it."

Tell raised the bow. Twang! The arrow flew through the air. There was a great shout from the people. What did it mean?

Tell had turned his face, for he was afraid he had shot his son. Then he felt a little arm around his neck. "Father, I am safe! The arrow went right through the center of the apple!"

That was why the people shouted. Even Gessler's men were glad. But Gessler was angry and would have sent Tell back to prison, if he had dared. But he saw that Tell had more friends than he.

"You may go free, now," he said, "But do not come in my way again."

The huntsman and his child went back to their home among the mountains, and the good wishes of all the people went with them.

Taken from *Baldwin's Readers*, Third Year © 1897

Dear Parents

This version of William Tell's story was taken from a Baldwin's Reader, published in 1897—proof that some stories are truly timeless. I hope you and your child enjoy this version of the story. Please remind your child that this is a story from European folklore and that it involves a dangerous, unrealistic situation that they should not attempt.

TIP OF THE WEEK

On state and national tests, students are often asked to infer information about characters from the stories in which they appear. To help your child practice this skill, ask him or her to choose three or four words to describe the main characters of the story, Tell and Gessler. Then ask your child why he or she thinks that—encouraging him or her to support the inferences with evidence from the text.

The Questions

List three words each to best describe Tell and Gessler:

Tell	Gessler
1. _____	1. _____
2. _____	2. _____
3. _____	3. _____

Now complete the following sentences using one word from each answer and some information from the story to justify your choice of words.

I think William Tell was _____ because _____

_____

I think Gessler was _____ because _____

_____

We have completed this assignment together.

_____   _____
        Child's Signature   Parent's Signature

Week-by-Week Homework for Building Reading Comprehension and Fluency
Scholastic Professional Books

Señor Coyote, the Judge

At the foot of a mountain, Señor Rattlesnake was sleeping in the sun. A big stone rolled down the mountain and landed right on top of Señor Rattlesnake! He was stuck.

He tried over and over again to get out from under the rock, but it was no use. Then along came Señor Rabbit.

"Hello," said Señor Rabbit. "I see you are trying to crawl under that stone."

"Don't make fun of me," said Señor Rattle-snake. "Help me. It hurts. Just roll this stone off, and I'll see you get a reward."

Señor Rabbit knew that the rattlesnake was not a friend. But the rabbit himself was kind and didn't like to see anyone unhappy.

"All right," he said. "But I don't want a reward."

He pushed and pushed and pushed. Finally the stone rolled off Señor Rattlesnake.

"Now," said Señor Rattlesnake. "About your reward."

"Oh, that's all right," answered Señor Rabbit. "I told you I don't want any."

"I think you do," said Señor Rattlesnake.

"What do you mean?" asked the rabbit.

"I mean that you get to be my dinner!" said the snake, coming at Señor Rabbit.

"Oh, no," said Señor Rabbit. "Do not eat me." He walked back.

"Yes, my friend," said the snake, following the rabbit. "I must have my dinner."

Just then, up came Señor Coyote. "What goes on here?" he asked.

Both the rabbit and the snake began talking at once, trying to tell their stories.

"Stop," said Señor Coyote. "You need a judge. And I will be it."

Señor Rabbit and Sénor Rattlesnake agreed.

Señor Rabbit began, "I came here and found Señor Rattlesnake under the stone. I pushed it off him. He offered me a reward, but I didn't want it. Now he wants to eat me!"

"Listen," said Señor Rattlesnake, "that is not true. I could have gotten out from under the stone at any time. I *like* it under there; it's cool. Señor Rabbit happened to come along. He's a fine dinner. And I have the right to eat him."

Señor Coyote thought a while.

"Let's see," he said at last. "We must be sure to have the right answer, my friends. Now you both say Señor Rattlesnake was under the stone. Right?"

"Yes," they both agreed.

"Very well," said Señor Coyote. "I must know just how everything was. Señor Rattlesnake, please come over here by the stone. Señor Rabbit and I will roll it on top of you. I'll know who's right, then."

The snake went over to the stone, and the other two rolled it on his back.

"Now," said Señor Coyote. "Is that the way you were, Señor Rattlesnake?"

"Yes," said the snake. He didn't seem happy.

"And that is the way you will stay," said Señor Coyote. "You have your reward for trying to eat Señor Rabbit."

And the two walked off. Señor Rattlesnake was left with lots of time to think about it.

By Ann Elwood.
Published by Globe Publishing Company.

Week-by-Week Homework for Building Reading Comprehension and Fluency
Scholastic Professional Books

Dear Parents

This delightful folk tale is from the southwestern United States and carries a moral about gratitude and trickery. I hope you enjoy listening to your child read this story out loud to you.

TIP OF THE WEEK

One of the most difficult things we ask students to do in interpreting literature is to "read between the lines," inferring information about characters and events that the author does not state outright. In the opening of this story, the rabbit says sarcastically, "I see you are trying to crawl under that stone." Young students often read something like this without realizing that the author is using the rabbit to make a funny comment. Even worse, students sometimes take this literally and think the snake was trying to crawl under the stone. Help your child understand these subtle messages by pointing them out as they are read.

The Questions

"Read between the lines" to answer the following questions:

1. How did the rattlesnake trick the rabbit? _____

_____

2. How did the coyote trick the rattlesnake? _____

_____

3. What is the moral of this story? _____

_____

4. What is the author's purpose in writing this story? _____

_____

We have completed this assignment together.

_____   _____
Child's Signature   Parent's Signature

39

The Hickory Toothpick

One winter we sure had a big snow. I was livin' up a ways on Pine Mountain, and one morning I tried to open the door, and I couldn't. The snow had piled up plumb over the house.

I kept my stove goin'. Had me a fairly good pile of wood in the house—and enough rations for a day or two. But after about four days my wood was gone, and the meat, too. The snow didn't seem to thaw much, and after I'd burned up all my shelves and a couple of chairs I knew I had to get out and find some firewood.

So I took the stovepipe down, knocked a few planks loose from around the fire-place flue, got my ax, and crawled out onto the roof and I finally made it out on top of all that snow. It was a big snowfall—plumb over the tops of all but the tallest trees.

But 'way up on one cliff of Pine Mountain there was one tree—a hicko-ry—the snow hadn't buried. So I headed for it. The crust was hard enough to hold me up as I went. I could see directly where other folks' houses were snowed under.

Got to that hickory tree finally and then I cut that tree. Went to trimmin' it. Piled up the limbs right careful, so's I'd have plenty of kindlin'. Oh, I saved every twig! But—don't you know!—when I hacked off that last limb, the main log jumped and slid top foremost down the south side of the mountain. There went my stovewood!

I watched it slitherin' down, faster and faster. It was goin' so fast it shot across the bottom and up Black Mountain it flew. I thought it 'uld go right up in the air and over yon' side of The Black. But it slowed down just at the top of the ridge, stopped with its top teeterin'—and here it came back. Scooted across where the river was and headed up The Pine again. Stopped right at me, and down across the valley it went again. Hit the bottom goin' so fast, it was smokin'. Went right back up Black Mountain, clean to the top, and back down this way again. Well, I watched it see-sawin' a few times, and finally gathered up that pile of brush and made it back to the house and started my fire—and forgot about the big log a'swayin' in the valley.

About a week later I finally heard, drip! drip! drip! So I shoved on the door, mashed the snow back, and got out. Snow was still about eight foot deep. I got my ax and headed for the nearest tree. Got me a good pile of wood in and fixed the fire till my little stove was red-hot.

Had to go fetch some meal and other rations. I was gettin' a little hungry. So I took off for the store at Putney.

I looked over the country and noticed a sort of trough there between the two mountains where that log had been slidin'. I went right down there. Couldn't see that hickory log at all. But when I got to the bottom of that trough I looked, and there—still slidin' back and forth just a few inches—was my log. And don't you know! With all that see-sawin' that log had worn down to the size of a toothpick. I leaned over and picked it up, stuck it in my pocket.

You may not believe me, but I've kept it to this day. There. Look at it yourself. Best toothpick I ever had.

From *Literature and Writing Workshop.*
Copyright © 1993 by Scholastic Inc. Used by permission.

Week-by-Week Homework for Building Reading Comprehension and Fluency
Scholastic Professional Books

Dear Parents

This lively tall tale about a hickory tree is sure to captivate your child— but only if he or she can understand the unusual language. This story is written in dialect, meaning that the words are spelled to reflect the way they're spoken, such as "I went shoppin'" instead of "I went shopping." This story requires you to read along with as well as listen to your child.

The Questions

Circle the following words in the story. Then on the line beside each word, write what you think each one means based on how it's used in the story. Do not copy a dictionary definition, but use your own words to describe its meaning in *this* story. These words could mean something very different if they were used in another story!

1. plumb _____

2. rations _____

3. thaw _____

4. trimmin' _____

5. see-sawin' _____

6. trough _____

We have completed this assignment together.

_____   _____
Child's Signature   Parent's Signature

Week-by-Week Homework for Building Reading Comprehension and Fluency
Scholastic Professional Books

How Big Is A Foot?

ONCE UPON A TIME there lived a King and his wife, the Queen. They were a happy couple for they had everything in the world. However . . . when the Queen's birthday came near, the King had a problem: What could he give to Someone who had Everything? The King thought and he thought and he thought. Until suddenly, he had an idea! HE WOULD GIVE THE QUEEN A BED. The Queen did not have a bed because at the time beds had not been invented. So even Someone who had Everything—did not have a bed.

The King called his Prime Minister and asked him to please have a bed made. The Prime Minister called the Chief Carpenter and asked him to please have a bed made. The Chief Carpenter called the apprentice and told him to make a bed. "How big is a bed?" asked the apprentice, who didn't know because at the time nobody had ever seen a bed. "How big is a bed?" the Carpenter asked the Prime Minister. "A good question," said the Prime Minister. And he asked the King, "HOW BIG IS A BED?" The King thought and he thought and he thought. Until suddenly he had an idea! THE BED MUST BE BIG ENOUGH TO FIT THE QUEEN.

The King called the Queen. He told her to put on her new pajamas and told her to lie on the floor. The King took off his shoes and with his big feet walked carefully around the Queen. He counted that the bed must be THREE FEET WIDE AND SIX FEET LONG to be big enough to fit the Queen. (Including the crown which the Queen sometimes liked to wear to sleep.)

The King said "thank you" to the Queen, and told the Prime Minister who told the Chief Carpenter, who told the apprentice: "The bed must be three feet wide and six feet long to be big enough to fit the Queen." (Including the crown which the Queen sometimes liked to wear to sleep.) The apprentice said "thank you" and took off his shoes, and with his little feet, he measured six feet long and three feet wide and made a bed for the Queen.

When the King saw the bed, he thought it was beautiful. He could not wait for the Queen's birthday. Instead, he called the Queen at once and told her to put on her new pajamas. Then he brought out the bed and told the Queen to try it. BUT the bed was much too small for the Queen.

The King was so angry that he immediately called the Prime Minister who called the Chief Carpenter who called the jailer who threw the apprentice into jail.

The apprentice was unhappy. WHY WAS THE BED TOO SMALL FOR THE QUEEN? He thought and he thought and he thought. Until suddenly he had an idea! A bed that was three king's feet wide and six king's feet long was naturally

Week-by-Week Homework for Building Reading Comprehension and Fluency
Scholastic Professional Books

bigger than a bed that was three apprentice feet wide and six apprentice feet long. "I CAN MAKE A BED TO FIT THE QUEEN IF I KNOW THE SIZE OF THE KING'S FOOT," he cried. He explained this to the jailer, who explained it to the Chief Carpenter, who explained it to the Prime Minister, who explained it to the King, who was much too busy to go to the jail. Instead, the King took off one shoe and called a famous sculptor. The sculptor made an exact copy of the King's foot. This was sent to the jail. The apprentice took the marble copy of the King's foot, and with it he measured three feet wide and six feet long and built a bed to fit the Queen! The bed was ready just in time for the Queen's birthday.

The King called the Queen and told her to put on her new pajamas. Then he brought out the New Bed and told the Queen to try it. THE BED FIT THE QUEEN PERFECTLY. (Including the crown which the Queen sometimes liked to wear to sleep.) It was without doubt the nicest gift that the Queen had ever received. The King was very happy. He immediately called the apprentice from jail and made him a royal prince.

He ordered a big parade, and all the people came out to cheer the little apprentice prince. And forever after, anyone who wanted to measure anything used a copy of the King's foot. And when someone said, "My bed is three feet wide," everyone knew exactly how big it was.

©1962 by Rolf Myller from *How Big is a Foot?* Atheneum Publishers

Dear Parents

Please listen to your child read this charming story out loud. Thanks for your continued support of your child's reading!

TIP OF THE WEEK

Many children's stories contain a pattern of sayings or events that contribute to the charm of the tale. "How Big Is A Foot?" contains both repetitive phrases and repetitive events. This is referred to as "story structure." Recognizing the structure of a story is often a key to understanding the events being described.

The Questions

List two repetitive phrases that are found in this story:

1. _____

_____

2. _____

_____

Use your own words to describe two repetitive events from the story:

1. _____

_____

2. _____

_____

We have completed this assignment together.

_____   _____
Child's Signature   Parent's Signature

Week-by-Week Homework for Building Reading Comprehension and Fluency
Scholastic Professional Books

Biography

Passages	Skill Focus	Standard
More Miracles for Helen Keller	❁ Separating main idea from supporting details	❁ Determines main idea ❁ Finds supporting details
Tazio Nuvolari, Racing Legend	❁ Separating fact from opinion	❁ Identifies fact, fiction, and opinion in text
Dr. Samuel Lee Kountz Jr., Kidney Specialist	❁ Determining main idea ❁ Finding supporting details ❁ Answering literal questions	❁ Determines main idea ❁ Finds supporting details ❁ Distinguishes between significant and minor details
William H. Cosby Jr.	❁ Recognizing print conventions	❁ Uses text features to enhance comprehension

*U*pper grade students are fascinated by stories of celebrities and famous figures. The articles presented here introduce them to some people with whom they might not be familiar—but who are certainly worth knowing! At the same time, students are practicing valuable reading skills that will come in handy at test-taking time: determining main ideas, finding supporting details, using context clues, separating fact and opinion, and recognizing print conventions.

Week-by-Week Homework for Building Reading Comprehension and Fluency
Scholastic Professional Books

More Miracles for Helen Keller

✓ **Skill focus:** Separating Main Idea From Supporting Details

In some states, questions concerning main idea can make up as much as 35 percent of the entire reading assessment, so it is vitally important that we spend extra time teaching this reading skill. In many of the activities in this book, students are asked to support their ideas with information from the text. To do this, they need to know which ideas are the main focus and which can be used as support.

This activity asks students to list ten important facts about Helen Keller. Remember that all of these facts should be from the text, although they can be inferences. Students should not add non-text information on reading assessments unless they are specifically asked to do so.

After students have listed the facts, they are asked to choose the three most important ones. These are the main ideas of the article. (This is slightly different from the summarizing activity, which is featured in the piece on Samuel Lee Kountz, page 53.) This activity should be repeated often with articles of increasing length.

Tazio Nuvolari, Racing Legend

✓ **Skill focus:** Separating Fact From Opinion

This fast-paced article on a racing legend brims with fascinating facts and outspoken opinion. Differentiating between fact and opinion is difficult for young readers, but by the upper elementary grades they should be able to distinguish between the two if the opinions are clearly stated or are their own. In the homework accompanying the article, identifying the opinions is more challenging because students must infer the opinion of the author. This task will probably be a new experience for most students, so you may want to emphasize that they are looking for the author's opinion—not their own—and tell them that they can infer the author's opinion from statements in the article.

In many state assessments, students are expected to respond in paragraph form explaining a fact or opinion instead of just answering a multiple-choice question. This activity is a good precursor to the more sophisticated kinds of test questions students will soon face.

It is important to note that at this level, students should begin to separate not only fact and opinion, but also fact, fiction, and opinion. For example, that the Grinch lived in a cave is a fact, even though it is in a fiction story. Students often have difficulty with this concept because they think that a "fact" is a true fact in life.

Dr. Samuel Lee Kountz Jr., Kidney Specialist

✓ **Skill focus:** Determining Main Idea, Finding Supporting Details, and Answering Literal Questions

This is a synopsis of one of a series of articles that can be found on the web site BlackHistory.com. This is a wonderful resource to enhance any study of African Americans or the sciences.

Although identifying the main idea of an article is relatively easy for adults, it is difficult for less experienced readers, who often include supporting details that are interesting to them or that they simply remember. One way to help students determine the main idea is to encourage them to summarize a piece in one sentence, as this activity asks students to do. Try this with fiction and nonfiction pieces to give kids lots of practice with this important skill. Remember that the main idea is also called the "focus," the "subject," and the "topic"; use these words synonymously in the classroom so that kids will recognize them on tests.

Follow-up: As you read and discuss various stories and articles in class, point out that writers often strive to capture the focus, or main idea, of their work in their title. Remind students to give titles to their own writing, which gives them practice at winnowing down the main idea to a few words. It also helps them to better answer those test questions that ask—as a way of getting to the main idea—"What would make a good title for this article?"

William H. Cosby Jr.

✓ **Skill focus:** Recognizing Print Conventions

Frequent discussions of conventions of print help students navigate all sorts of texts. What may appear as little squiggles to students help authors convey their meaning—and authors rely upon their readers to interpret these signs. Try asking students to help you create a chart of all the conventions of print they can list: commas, quotation marks, underlining, capitals, dashes, indentations, apostrophes, and so forth. Kids will be amazed at the long list of conventions they already know! Encourage students to pay attention to each of these and to be on the look-out for new ones because they drastically affect the meaning of the printed word.

Follow-up: The poem "The Flotz," by Jack Prelutzky, is a great addition to any study of print conventions. Prelutzky's delightful creature loves to gobble dots, dashes, periods, commas, and any other punctuation he can find on the pages of children's writing. Read this engaging poem aloud with your class. After that, whenever students omit punctuation, you can say, "I guess the Flotz is at it again!" Invoking the Flotz is a gentle and fun reminder for students to use punctuation to make their meaning clear.

More Miracles for Helen Keller

Imagine the most famous person you know. Michael Jordan. Britney Spears. Prince William. Now think of this: Not one of them is as famous as Helen Keller was in her day.

Back in the late 1800s, nobody believed that blind or deaf people could lead normal lives. Most were sent away from their homes. They lived in bleak schools that were more like prisons than places to learn and grow. Few people believed that a person who was both blind and deaf could ever learn to communicate. But Annie Sullivan believed she could teach 7-year-old Helen Keller language.

When Annie first met Helen in 1887, Helen was wild and angry. She spoke by grunting and screaming. Nobody, not even Helen's parents, believed Annie would succeed. And when she did succeed, news of this miracle spread far.

Helen often said that she had spent her early childhood in a "dungeon of silence" and loneliness. Freed from this dungeon by Annie, Helen blossomed. By the age of 10, Helen was able to write and read Braille—an alphabet system based on raised dots that people can feel on a page. In addition to English, Helen also learned French and Greek. She even learned to talk clearly enough so that Annie could understand her.

People all over the country wanted to witness Helen's miracle themselves. Writer Mark Twain, inventor Alexander Graham Bell, and President Grover Cleveland were just a few of the people who met with young Helen. When she got older, she went to Radcliffe College, the most selective women's college in the country. Annie went to all of Helen's lectures with her, and translated them into sign language. Helen graduated with honors.

She became an author, writing 13 books and hundreds of articles. She and Annie traveled around the world. She learned to ride a horse and a bike. When she died, just before her 88th birthday, she had become one of America's great heros.

"Life," Helen once said, "is either a daring adventure or nothing."

By Lauren Tarshis, Editor, *Storyworks*
Reprinted from *Storyworks*, October 2000

Dear Parents

The story of Helen Keller is inspiring and reminds us all not to set limits on ourselves. If your child is curious to learn more about Keller after reading this short article, check out the following: _Helen Keller_ by Kennis Wepman, American Women of Achievement series (Chelsea House, 1987); _Helen Keller and Helen Keller's Teacher_ by Margaret Davisdon (Scholastic Inc., 1997); _Story of My Life_ by Helen Keller (Doubleday, 1991); and _Out of Darkness, The Story of Louis Braille_ by Russell Freedman (Scholastic Inc., 1997).

TIP OF THE WEEK

As your child is reading this aloud, if she mispronounces a word, omits words, or adds words, try not to correct her. See if your child is actually "listening to herself read." If she is, she will hear that what she has read does not make sense and will immediately "self-correct" without your interference. Of course, if a child does not hear the error, we do need to intervene and offer guidance. The biggest issue here is teaching the child to be engaged in her reading, to listen to herself, and to realize that all reading should make sense.

The Questions

Write ten facts about Helen Keller:

1.   6.

2.   7.

3.   8.

4.   9.

5.   10.

Now circle the three facts that you think are the most important ones that someone would need to know if they had never heard of this remarkable lady. These are the main ideas of the article. All of the rest of the facts you have listed are supporting details.

We have completed this assignment together.

_____ _____
Child's Signature   Parent's Signature

Tazio Nuvolari, Racing Legend

When you think of race car drivers, who comes to mind? Jeff Gordon? Richard Petty? Michael Andretti? Michael Schumacher? How about *Tazio Nuvolari?* (TA–zee–o New–vo–LAR–ee) Never heard of him? Tazio Nuvolari is considered by many to be the finest race car driver that ever got behind the wheel of a car. He was truly a "legend in his own time."

Tazio was born in 1892 near Mantua, Italy. He began racing Bianchi motorcycles when he was about 28. While he was the Italian motorcycle champion, he had a bad crash and broke both of his legs, but he still wanted to race. They put old-fashioned heavy plaster casts on both legs and told him he couldn't walk for at least a month. But Tazio would not listen. He got his mechanics to tie him onto his bike so that he couldn't put his feet on the ground. Then two mechanics stood, one on each side of him, during the start of the race and promised to catch him at the end. The legend of Tazio began when he won that race.

In 1924 Tazio bought a car called a *Bugatti* (Boo-GA-ti) and turned to car racing. For years, he raced particularly hard against his ex-partner and greatest rival, *Achille Varzi,* (A-KEEL VAR -zee), who had much more money, better equipment, more helpers, and much faster cars. In 1930 the two racers were both in a famous Italian race called the Mille Miglia (which means "one-thousand mile" race). Because the race is so long, they actually drive all through the night. Tazio knew that Varzi was much faster and would win for sure. Luckily it was a full moon. Tazio turned off his headlights and raced his Alfa P2 through the winding mountain roads in the gray moonlit night. Varzi, seeing no one in his rear-view mirror, assumed that he was winning the race by a long way, so he slowed down. About a mile from the end of the race, Tazio laughed, flicked on his headlights, and powered right past the surprised Varzi to win the race. The legend continued!

Once Tazio was in Ireland to drive in a race, and they asked him how he liked the brakes on his MG. He replied that he didn't know. He hadn't used them during the race. (Remember that these were races over winding dirt roads in the mountains!!)

During practice for a race, Tazio had a serious accident and was sent to the hospital to recover. When no one was looking, he escaped from the hospital and took a taxi to the racetrack. He won again.

Tazio's unbelievable feats on the track never seemed to stop. One time when he was 53, he was racing a car and the steering wheel came off in his hand. Tazio continued to race holding the steering wheel in one hand and the steering column (the part that goes down under the dashboard) in the other.

When Tazio died in 1953, thousands of people attended his funeral and the racing community around the world mourned his death. It was said of Tazio Nuvolari, "A man like that won't be born again." He made himself a legend.

By Mary Rose

Week-by-Week Homework for Building Reading Comprehension and Fluency
Scholastic Professional Books

Dear Parents

Who can help being fascinated by race-car drivers who zoom around tracks at 200 miles per hour for 500 miles! What many of us fail to realize is that car racing has been around for a very long time; from the first moment that more than one car sputtered to life, people have been trying to see which could go faster. This article is about a race-car driver from the 1920s who made marks in the sport that will probably never be eclipsed. I hope you enjoy reading about Tazio Nuvolari.

The Questions

1. Use your own words (do not copy sentences from the text) to write two facts about Tazio Nuvolari:

   1. _____

   2. _____

2. Use your own words (do not copy sentences from the text) to write two of the author's opinions about Tazio Nuvolari:

   1. _____

   2. _____

3. What was the author's purpose in writing this piece? _____

   _____

   _____

We have completed this assignment together.

_____   _____
Child's Signature   Parent's Signature

Week-by-Week Homework for Building Reading Comprehension and Fluency
Scholastic Professional Books

Dr. Samuel Lee Kountz Jr., Kidney Specialist

Dr. Samuel Lee Kountz Jr. set a goal for himself when he was only eight years old. At that very young age, he decided to become a doctor. Thank goodness he didn't stop with just that one goal! Our lives may depend on his contribution to medical science, even if our kidneys are functioning perfectly.

Dr. Kountz obtained a master's degree in biochemistry at the University of Arkansas, Fayetteville, and was one of the first African Americans admitted to its medical school (University of Arkansas for Medical Sciences, Little Rock, 1958). Medical science was just beginning to perform transplants—taking an organ from a dying person and "hooking it up" inside of another. One of the biggest problems with this kind of procedure was that the dying person was not usually near the person who needed a new kidney. Getting the kidney to the patient was difficult, because it had to be kept clean and fresh or it would kill the person receiving it! Kountz became an authority on kidney transportation, and he even performed an operation live on the NBC *Today* show.

But transporting the kidney to the patient was only one of many problems with transplanting organs. The body of the person who gets the new organ doesn't really know that the organ is there to help out. It is the body's natural process to reject or try to kill anything that is in it that doesn't belong there. This is where Dr. Kountz helped out again. He spent many years helping to determine how to give special drugs to the person with the new kidney so that the body would stop trying to get rid of it. These drugs are called "anti-rejection drugs" and they are dangerous and very powerful. The dosage that is given to the patient must be monitored very closely or the patient will die. Dr. Kountz specialized in learning just how to manage the amount of drugs that a person needs and how to constantly change and adjust the medicines so that they will be just right for the person with the new organ.

He is important to all of us because of his research in this area. As transplants become more and more common in these modern times, we may need his research and studies to help ourselves or someone we love to be able to have an organ transplant.

Dr. Kountz established the largest kidney transplant research and training program in the country at the University of California, San Francisco. He died in 1981.

By Mary Rose

Week-by-Week Homework for Building Reading Comprehension and Fluency
Scholastic Professional Books

Dear Parents

Dr. Samuel Lee Kountz was a pioneer in kidney transplant surgery, a determined man who followed through on his childhood dream to become a doctor. The accompanying article describes his many accomplishments and contains some challenging vocabulary; please help your child understand what a transplant is and what anti-rejection drugs are.

The Questions

1. State the main idea of this passage in your own words: _____
_____
_____
_____

2. List at least three supporting details found in this article about Dr. Samuel Lee Kountz:

1. _____
_____

2. _____
_____

3. _____
_____

We have completed this assignment together.

_____   _____
Child's Signature   Parent's Signature

Week-by-Week Homework for Building Reading Comprehension and Fluency
Scholastic Professional Books

William H. Cosby Jr.

On July 12, 1937, William H. Cosby Jr. was born in Philadelphia, Pennsylvania. His dad, William H. Cosby Sr. was in the Navy and his mom worked as a maid. But when William was only ten, his brother died and his dad left the family, and they suddenly had very little money. There was another little brother to take care of, so William began to help out at home and also started working in a grocery store.

William soon became known as just "Bill." He was not a very good student, but he was a good athlete. He dropped out of school in the tenth grade and went into the Navy, like his dad. Then he realized he had made a mistake by quitting school, so he finished his high school degree while he was in the service. When he got out of the Navy, he got a scholarship to play football and run track at Temple University. He had decided to become a teacher, but while he was still in college, he began to realize that the thing he was best at was making people laugh. He finally decided to be a stand-up comedian. This means that he was going to take a microphone, stand in front of a crowd of people, and do nothing but talk—no tricks, no songs. Just talk and make them laugh. And laugh they did. Soon Bill was performing his act from New York to California.

Back then there were very few black men on television. In 1965, Bill became the first black to costar in a dramatic (serious) series, a show called *I Spy. I Spy* was very successful, but although Bill loved being on television, he wasn't doing what he liked most—making people laugh. And Bill still had that nagging desire to be a teacher. Since he wasn't a teacher, he decided to play one on *The Bill Cosby Show* in 1969. He also made recordings of his comedy routines and won eight Grammy awards for them.

Then Bill created a new television show with messages for children, *Fat Albert and the Cosby Kids,* which was a huge hit. Fat Albert was a cartoon character that tried to teach children to be honest, loyal, and caring. Still pursing his dream of being a teacher, he returned to college and got both a masters degree and a doctorate degree in education. But he didn't work in a classroom—he decided to do his educating on television. His next big adventure was to read for Reading Rainbow and to start *The Cosby Show,* which became a hit its very first season. The lovable Huxtable family on this show faced all kinds of problems with their children but dealt with them with grace thanks to Bill's common sense and humor. He became a role model for many fathers who were trying to cope with teenagers and work in a modern world. He even wrote a book, *Fatherhood,* that became a best seller—not bad for a guy who dropped out of high school in the tenth grade!

By Mary Rose

54

Dear Parents

Many of you fondly remember *The Cosby Show* featuring the Huxtable family. But do you know the real story behind the popular comedian Bill Cosby? Have fun as you listen to your child read this short biography out loud to you.

The Questions

Use a crayon, colored pencil, or highlighter to help answer these questions:

1. Circle or highlight the word *dramatic* in this article. Notice that it is followed by a word in parentheses. What is this word and why did the author put it there?

   _____

   _____

2. Circle or highlight the phrase *stand-up comedian*. Where does the author explain

   what a stand-up comedian is? _____

   _____

3. Circle or highlight the two places where there is a dash followed by three or four words. What is explained by the words following each dash? _____

   _____

   _____

4. Circle or highlight all of the italicized words. What do they have in common?

   _____

   _____

We have completed this assignment together.

_____   _____
Child's Signature   Parent's Signature

Week-by-Week Homework for Building Reading Comprehension and Fluency
Scholastic Professional Books

Poetry

Passages	Skill Focus	Standard
Ice Can Scream	● Identifying verbs	● Recognizes parts of speech
School Daze Rap Sick	● Identifying theme	● Uses appropriate literary terminology ● Identifies characteristics of literary genres (poetry) ● Reads fluently
Mary and Her Little Lamb	● Relating personal experience to text	● Recognizes that time period affects language and events of story ● Compares literature to events in own life
Casey at the Bat	● Sequencing story events	● Arranges events in chronological order

*M*ore and more state assessments require students to respond to poetry as a reading passage. At the same time, poems are perfect for teaching literary elements and reading strategies because they are short, complete works, often with rhyme and a rhythm that appeal to young readers. The skills taught in this section range from identifying verbs to identifying theme, illustrating the many possibilities of teaching with poems and giving students much-needed practice responding to poetry.

Ice Can Scream

Skill focus: Identifying Verbs

Although this poem is short, it is certainly not easily understood. Once students have had a chance to read it several times and explore the verbs in it (as the homework asks), take some class time to discuss the concept of personification (giving an inanimate object human characteristics—in this case, giving ice the ability to scream or shout) and how the author uses it to characterize the ice. Ask students if they think the author likes or dislikes winter and ice. Encourage students to support their opinion using examples from the poem. (For example: The author dislikes the ice because it is "yelling, howling, screaming," all unpleasant noises. The author likes the ice because it has secrets and it is powerful and brings winter.)

Understanding personification, inferring opinion, and supporting ideas with evidence from a text are high-level thinking skills that help students understand and respond to poetry. Encourage students to try out these skills on other poems they read, too.

School Daze Rap and Sick

Skill focus: Identifying Theme

These outrageous poems are always kid favorites, and they lend themselves well to a first discussion of theme, an idea or message an author expresses in his or her work. The authors' thoughts on school come through loud and clear, and kids easily pick up on them and eagerly discuss them. Help students differentiate between the theme of a poem and the events that happen in a poem. In this pair of poems, the theme is that kids often don't want to go to school. But the events are clearly different. Starting off small—with short, easy poems and stories— helps students solidify their understanding of theme before we ask them to tackle it in more complex works.

Remember that *theme* is usually a term used for fiction stories, but theme, main idea, focus, topic, and subject are really all the same thing—the big idea that a story, article, or poem is about. Use all these terms so students are familiar with them when test time rolls around.

Mary and Her Little Lamb

✓ **Skill focus:** Relating Personal Experience to Text

Although decoding words, retelling events, and answering literal questions are all things proficient readers can do, we hope that our students will do much more. Good readers take what they read one step further, relating what they've read to their own life and bringing their own experience to the text for a more complete understanding of it.

The activity accompanying this reading encourages kids to connect their own experience with animals to Mary's. If children have had a dog or cat follow them around the house or down the street, Mary's experience with the lamb will be more vivid for them. This activity is a first step toward getting kids to draw on their own experiences to enrich their reading.

Casey at the Bat

✓ **Skill focus:** Sequencing Story Events

This classic poem is a great way to familiarize students with our national pastime and give them practice at retelling stories and sequencing events. The plot of this story is really quite simple, and, with the help of a parent, students should be able to easily understand what has occurred in the poem.

Even though we still refer to baseball as "our national pastime," many students will not realize that one point is scored for each "run" in baseball or understand what it means to get "three outs." They may have missed the whole possibility that the Mudville nine could have won the game if Casey had hit a homer. You may want to have a baseball discussion before sending this home or after the homework pages are returned to your classroom. Try rereading the poem aloud in class and discussing the scoring and the game as a whole. Be sure to emphasize the last stanza, as it is the most important and is often found in literary references that the child will probably encounter in the future.

Ice Can Scream

Ice can call,
Ice can yell
Secrets no one
Else can tell.

Ice can yell,
Ice can howl,
Naming winter's
Weather foul.

Ice can howl,
Ice can wail,
Counting up
Each storm and gale.

Ice can wail,
Ice can shriek
Till the land
Is winter-bleak.

Ice can shriek,
Ice can scream
Straight across
The autumn dream.

Ice can scream,
Ice can shout:
Winter in
And autumn out.

From *Once Upon Ice and Other
Frozen Poems* selected by Jane Yolen.
Published by Boyds Mills Press, 1997.

59

Week-by-Week Homework for Building Reading Comprehension and Fluency
Scholastic Professional Books

Dear Parents

Read this dramatic poem about ice out loud with your child. Then ask your child to read it out loud alone as you listen. Reading a poem many times is enjoyable and helps us appreciate its sound, rhythm, and meaning. You may want to discuss how the poet treats the ice like a person, having it do things humans can do, such as yell. This technique is called personification. Most of all, enjoy the strong language and rhythm of the poem.

The Questions

Read the poem a third time. List all of the verbs—action words—that you can find. Can you think of some you would use that the poet did not? Add them to your list.

scream

shout

_____   _____   _____

_____   _____   _____

_____   _____   _____

_____   _____   _____

Bonus: Can you find a pattern that the verbs follow in the poem from stanza to stanza?

_____

_____

We have completed this assignment together.

_____   _____
Child's Signature   Parent's Signature

School Daze Rap

Woke up at eight-oh no, I overslept!

I ran for the bus, but the bus had left.

I raced to school, I really, really buzzed,

But then I forgot where my classroom was.

Finally found it, opened the door—

My teacher turned into a dinosaur!

The dinosaur roared, "Sit down at your desk!

Pick up your pencil, 'cause we're having a test!"

All the kids were staring, sitting in their rows,

I looked down and saw I'd forgotten my clothes!

The dinosaur frowned and started to shake me,

turned into my mom, who was trying to wake me.

"Hey, sleepyhead, Tommy's here to play,

Why aren't you up? It's Saturday!"

From *Lunch Money* by Carol Diggory Shields.
Copyright © 1995 by Carol Diggory Shields.
Used by permission of Dutton Children's Books, an
imprint of Penguin Putnam Books for Young Readers,
a Division of Penguin Putnam, Inc.

Sick

"I cannot go to school today,"
Said little Peggy Ann McKay.
"I have the measles and the mumps,
A gash, a rash and purple bumps.
My mouth is wet, my throat is dry,
I'm going blind in my right eye.
My tonsils are a big as rocks,
I've counted sixteen chicken pox
And there's one more—that's seventeen,
And don't you think my face looks green?
My leg is cut, my eyes are blue—
It might be instamatic flu.
I cough and sneeze and gasp and choke,
I'm sure that my left leg is broke—
My hip hurts when I move my chin,
My belly button's caving in,
My back is wrenched, my ankle's sprained,
My 'pendix pains each time it rains.
My nose is cold, my toes are numb,
I have a sliver in my thumb.
My neck is stiff, my voice is weak,
I hardly whisper when I speak.
My tongue is filling up my mouth,
I think my hair is falling out.
My elbow's bent, my spine ain't straight,
My temperature is one-o-eight.
My brain is shrunk, I cannot hear
There is a hole inside my ear.
I have a hangnail, and my heart is—what?
What's that? What's that you say?
You say today is . . . Saturday?
G'bye, I'm going out to play!"

From *Where the Sidewalk Ends* by Shel Silverstein.
Copyright © 1974 by Evil Eye Music, Inc.
Reprinted by permission of HarperCollins Children's Books.

Dear Parents

You and your child are sure to laugh at these rib-tickling poems about school life. Please read each poem aloud at least twice, enjoying the rhyming patterns and rhythms of the two pieces.

TIP OF THE WEEK

Building Fluency Short, fun rhyming poems are ideally suited for reading over and over again, a practice that helps kids read more smoothly, or fluently. Encourage your child to read these poems several times.

Identifying Theme A theme is an idea a writer is trying to express through his or her work. Ask your child to retell each poem and talk about what ideas, or themes, come through.

The Questions

1. Both of these poems are written in rhyming couplets. That means that each pair of lines ends with rhyming words, like "today, McKay." Find two sets of rhyming words from each poem and write them here:

   "School Daze Rap"   "Sick"

   _____ , _____   _____ , _____

   _____ , _____   _____ , _____

2. The themes of these two poems are also similar. Think about what happens in each poem. Then use a complete sentence to explain the theme the poems share.

   _____

   _____

3. These poems are also different. Think about the events of each poem. Use a complete sentence to explain one way the two poems are different.

   _____

   _____

We have completed this assignment together.

_____   _____
Child's Signature   Parent's Signature

Week-by-Week Homework for Building Reading Comprehension and Fluency
Scholastic Professional Books

Mary and Her Little Lamb

Mary had a little lamb,
Its fleece was white as snow,
And everywhere that Mary went,
The lamb was sure to go.

He followed her to school one day;
That was against the rule;
It made the children laugh and play,
To see a lamb at school.

And so the teacher turned him out;
But still he lingered near,
And waited patiently about,
Till Mary did appear.

And then he ran to her, and laid
His head upon her arm,
As if he said, "I'm not afraid,
You'll keep me from all harm."

"What makes the lamb love Mary so?"
The eager children cry;
"O, Mary loves the lamb, you know,"
The teacher did reply.

"And you, each gentle animal
To you, for life, may bind,
And make it follow at your call,
If you are always kind."

Week-by-Week Homework for Building Reading Comprehension and Fluency
Scholastic Professional Books

Mary and Her Little Lamb (cont.)

Every school child has heard this rhyme, but did you know that there really was a Mary and she really did have a lamb? Here is the true story of this famous poem. In 1806 Mary Elizabeth Sawyer was born in Sterling, Massachusetts, on a farm where her family raised many animals. One cold morning, she went to the barn with her father and found that two lambs had been born in the night. One had been abandoned by its mother and was nearly dead of the cold and of starvation. She talked her father into letting her take the creature into the house. There she patiently warmed and fed the little lamb and by the next morning it could stand up. It learned to drink milk and would follow Mary around everywhere.

As the lamb grew, Mary regularly combed and bathed it and treated it much as a child today would treat a favorite puppy. Because there were not many children around for playmates, Mary used to dress the lamb in clothes and play with it like a doll.

When Mary was about nine years old, she and her brother Nat decided to take the lamb to school. As always, the lamb followed close behind her. When they got to school, Mary put the lamb under her chair and covered her with a blanket and it went to sleep. When the teacher called on Mary to come to the front of the room to read, there was a *clatter, clatter, clatter* and the lamb rose to go with her. Mary was mortified! The teacher, Miss Polly Kimball, laughed out loud, as did all of the children, but Mary was ashamed. The lamb spent the rest of the morning in a shed and Mary took her home at lunchtime.

John Roulstone had been visiting the school that morning and had heard about the incident with the lamb; the next day he arrived on horseback to give Mary a slip of paper that had the original three stanzas of the poem he had written.

Mary's lamb lived for several years and was regularly sheered for its wool. Mary's mother had knitted a pair of stockings from the lamb's fleece and years after the poem became famous, Mary donated these stockings to a group that was raising money to preserve the Old South Church in Boston. On small cards Mary wrote, "Knitted yarn from the first fleece of Mary's Little Lamb," followed by her signature, Mary E. Sawyer, and the date. Those cards, along with Mary's personal retelling of her famous story, helped to raise hundreds of dollars to preserve the church.

Those cards can still be seen at museums such as the Henry Ford museum in Michigan, and can be purchased at special antique auctions. The fun of Mary's lamb's adventure at school still lives on for children today.

By Mary Rose

Week-by-Week Homework for Building Reading Comprehension and Fluency
Scholastic Professional Books

Dear Parents

The first few lines of this nursery rhyme will be familiar, but did you know that there were five more stanzas and that this is a true story? Have fun as you and your child read this poem and article out loud. Like most poetry, this piece should be read more than once to truly appreciate the rhythm and enjoy the rhymes.

TIP OF THE WEEK

Please help your child read the poem at least three times, and then ask him or her to retell the story to you in his or her own words. Retelling a story demonstrates comprehension, and many tests assess comprehension this way.

The question section of this activity asks students draw upon their personal experience with pets. If your child has never had a pet, help him or her answer the last question by talking about a friend's, neighbor's, or relative's pet and using that animal to write about.

The Questions

Please use more than one sentence to answer each of these questions:

1. Why did the lamb follow Mary everywhere she went? _____

   _____

2. What did the other children think about the lamb? How do you know? _____

   _____

   _____

3. Was it a good idea to take the lamb to school? Why? _____

   _____

   _____

4. On the back of this page, write a short paragraph about a time that you had a pet to take care of. Tell how you played with the pet and how you could tell that it liked you.

We have completed this assignment together.

_____   _____
Child's Signature   Parent's Signature

Week-by-Week Homework for Building Reading Comprehension and Fluency
Scholastic Professional Books

Casey at the Bat

Based on the classic American poem by Ernest Lawrence Thayer

The outlook wasn't brilliant for the Mudville nine that day;
The score stood four to two with but one inning more to play.
And then, when Cooney died at first, and Barrows did the same,
A sickly silence fell upon the patrons of the game.

A straggling few got up to go in deep despair. The rest
Clung to that hope which springs eternal in the human breast;
They thought, if only Casey could get a whack at that
We'd put up even money now, with Casey at the bat.

But Flynn preceded Casey, as did also Jimmy Blake,
And the former was a lulu and the latter was a cake;
So upon that stricken multitude grim melancholy sat,
For there seemed but little chance of Casey's getting to the bat.

But Flynn let drive a single, to the wonderment of all,
And Blake, the much despised, tore the cover off the ball,
And when the dust had lifted, and men saw what had occurred,
There was Jimmy safe at second, and Flynn a-hugging third.

Then from five thousand throats and more there rose a lusty yell;
It rumbled through the valley, it rattled in the dell,
It knocked upon the mountain and recoiled upon the flat,
For Casey, mighty Casey, was advancing to the bat.

There was ease in Casey's manner as he stepped into his place;
There was pride in Casey's bearing and a smile on Casey's face.
And when, responding to the cheers, he lightly doffed his hat,
No stranger in the crowd could doubt 'twas Casey at the bat.

Week-by-Week Homework for Building Reading Comprehension and Fluency
Scholastic Professional Books

Ten thousand eyes were on him as he rubbed his hands with dirt;
Five thousand tongues applauded when he wiped them on his shirt;
Then while the writhing pitcher ground the ball into his hip,
Defiance gleamed from Casey's eye, a sneer curled Casey's lip.

And now the leather-covered sphere came hurtling through the air,
And Casey stood a-watching it in haughty grandeur there.
Close by the sturdy batsman the ball unheeded sped;
"That ain't my style," said Casey. "Strike one," the umpire said.

From the benches, black with people, there went up a muffled roar.
Like the beating of the storm waves on a stern and distant shore.
"Kill him! Kill the umpire!" shouted someone on the stand.
And it's likely they'd have killed him had not Casey raised his hand.

With a smile of Christian charity great Casey's visage shone;
He stilled the rising tumult, he bade the game go on;
He signaled to the pitcher and once more the spheroid flew;
But Casey still ignored it, and the umpire said, "Strike two."

"Fraud!" cried the maddened thousands, and echo answered "Fraud!"
But one scornful look from Casey and the audience was awed;
They saw his face grow stern and cold, they saw his muscles strain,
And they knew that Casey wouldn't let that ball go by again.

The sneer is gone from Casey's lip, his teeth are clenched in hate,
He pounds with cruel violence his bat upon the plate;
And now the pitcher holds the ball, and now he lets it go,
And now the air is shattered by the force of Casey's blow.

Oh, somewhere in this favored land the sun is shining bright,
The band is playing somewhere, and somewhere hearts are light;
And somewhere men are laughing, and somewhere children shout,
But there is no joy in Mudville—
Might Casey
Has struck out.

Reprinted from *Storyworks*, April/May 1996

Week-by-Week Homework for Building Reading Comprehension and Fluency
Scholastic Professional Books

Dear Parents

"Casey at the Bat" is longer than most of our readings, but I hope you will enjoy it so much that you don't mind! The classic poem should be a standard for upper elementary students who, as they turn more and more to games like soccer and bike motorcross, are losing their familiarity with our national pastime. Please help your child to read the poem out loud and understand the events that occur.

TIP OF THE WEEK

As you discuss the poem, help your child place the events in the proper sequence, consulting the text as necessary. You can use these questions to prompt your child:

* How many innings are in a baseball game? What inning is it at the beginning of the poem?
* How many outs are there for each team's turn at bat?
* What did Cooney and Barrows do?
* How many outs are there now?
* What did Flynn and Blake do when they were at bat?
* How many points does Mudville need to win?
* Why does Casey need to hit a home run?

The Questions

List four events of this poem in the proper sequence:

1. _____

_____

2. _____

_____

3. _____

_____

4. _____

_____

We have completed this assignment together.

_____   _____
Child's Signature   Parent's Signature

Week-by-Week Homework for Building Reading Comprehension and Fluency
Scholastic Professional Books

Science

Passages	Skill Focus	Standard
Star Trek!	● Using test-taking strategies—multiple choice questions	● Uses text features to enhance comprehension
Arctic Disaster!	● Comparing and contrasting	● Recognizes use of compare and contrast
Zapped!	● Recognizing print conventions—interpreting bulleted information	● Uses text features to monitor comprehension
Antarctic Facts	● Categorizing information	● Identifies relevant supporting details
A Crayon Is Born	● Rereading text	● Makes inferences and draws conclusions regarding story elements
Bananas!!	● Recognizing persuasive techniques	● Recognizes when text is intended to persuade

*U*pper grade students love discovering things about their world. They're fascinated with how things work and where they come from. These articles will intrigue your students as well as give them practice with important reading skills.

Star Trek!

✓ **Skill focus:** Using Test-taking Strategies—Multiple Choice Questions

Students encounter multiple choice questions throughout their academic career, so it's only fair that we teach them strategies for tackling this type of test item. The strategies are summarized for parents in the tip:

* Read the questions first to set a purpose for reading.
* Read all four answers—even if you're sure that the first or second one is correct.
* Go back to the story and scan for a clue word or date to verify that an answer is correct.
* Look for clue words such as *least, never, most,* and *main,* which limit the scope of the question and can help eliminate incorrect answers.
* Consider the whole article when choosing alternative titles.

Take a few extra minutes to help students talk about the alternative, incorrect answers. Have them find justification for the correct answer in the text and high-light or circle it. It's just as important that students understand why certain responses are incorrect as it is to know the correct answer.

Arctic Disaster!

✓ **Skill focus:** Comparing and Contrasting

Comparing and contrasting can be challenging for students, so providing guided practice with pieces having obvious comparisons—like this piece on Arctic exploration—is very helpful. Encourage kids to practice on fiction they read, too; they can compare setting, character traits, or relationships at two points in a story or between two different stories. Using graphic organizers, such as a Venn diagram, can help students organize their thoughts as they make their comparisons.

Zapped!

✓ **Skill focus:** Recognizing Print Conventions—Interpreting Bulleted Information

There are two skills presented in this lesson: realizing that bullets usually represent a list of important information and learning to pay particular attention to the first sentence in a bulleted item. Students will see bullets in textbooks, articles, and even advertisements, so it is important for them to understand the type of information they present. Students can also learn to use bullets to present information in a report, presentation, or poster.

Antarctic Facts

 Skill focus: Categorizing Information

Students often read articles without connecting the various pieces of information they find. The assignment accompanying "Antarctic Facts" gives students a strategy for categorizing information—they learn to highlight similar pieces of information with the same color marker. This activity gives students a purpose for reading, is fun, and helps students begin to see relationships among pieces of information in an article. In this first activity, you provide the categories, but in subsequent practice, students will learn to devise their own categories from the kinds of information they're reading about.

A Crayon Is Born

Skill focus: Rereading Text

This activity asks students to cull information from a nonfiction passage, answering literal and inferential questions. Encourage students to go back to the text to support their responses to the inferential questions as well as double-check their answers to the literal ones. Returning to the text is an important test-taking strategy as well as a valuable skill when reading complex informational texts.

Bananas

Skill focus: Recognizing Persuasive Techniques

Most state assessments do not ask students to write persuasive essays until middle school, but many expect them to recognize the techniques used by persuasive writers. This short article uses several of them, such as getting the reader interested in the mundane; providing historical background; and convincing readers that their lives will be better if only they do this one thing.

Follow-up: Try to get your students to look objectively at cartoons and at ads in magazines and newspapers. See if they can find the exaggerations and separate them from the facts about the products.

Star Trek!

A Brand-New Space Laboratory Is Making History

Years ago, someone had an idea that was out of this world. What if countries from around the globe could get together and build a gigantic spacecraft? The craft would be an enormous moving laboratory that would orbit the Earth. Teams of astronauts from different countries could live on that craft, working together to conduct important scientific experiments. Imagine what the world could learn about space! Imagine how great it would be to have countries working together!

Some people said it couldn't be done. But as you read this, that fantastic idea is becoming a reality. The International Space Station (known as ISS) is currently flying around, 220 miles above the Earth. It is, in fact, the third-brightest object in the night sky, after the moon and Venus. In November 2000, an American astronaut and two Russian *cosmonauts* blasted into space to become the first people to live at the station.

How did it happen?

The ISS, which will be completed in 2004, is being constructed like a gigantic Lego airship. Large pieces, called *modules* (MOJ-oolz), are rocketed into space. Astronauts connect the pieces on risky space walks while moving at speeds up to 17,500 miles per hour. That's like trying to build a car while it's speeding around a track! The crews load supplies into the different modules and connect wiring so computer data and electricity can flow between modules.

The ISS isn't the most luxurious place; the living module is about as long as your average classroom. But astronauts will find everything they need to survive in space. The thick walls will protect astronauts from space temperatures, which can rise to 250F and drop to –250F. Breathable air is piped through the station from special tanks. Water is brought up in tanks, and then recycled through filters. (Don't gross out, but even astronaut urine is filtered and used for drinking. It's cleaner than most tap water!)

Certainly life in space has its dangers. Many astronauts worry the most about space *debris* (duh-BREE)—junk from old spacecrafts and satellites—and rocks from deep space. If even a *tiny* object hits the station, the force could cause catastrophic damage.

For the men and women who train for years to become astronauts, nothing compares with the excitement of going into space. "I've wanted to be an astronaut since the fourth grade," says Jerry Ross, an American astronaut who has flown on five missions and "can't wait" to join another ISS mission. "The risks are a small price for the experience of going into space. It's more spectacular than you can imagine," Jerry told us. "And I really believe that what we will discover there will be enormously important for mankind."

By Lauren Tarshis, Editor, *Storyworks*
Reprinted from *Storyworks*, November/December 2000

73

Dear Parents

This week's reading homework is about the International Space Station. Listen to your child read the article out loud and discuss the more difficult words (such as cosmonauts, modules, and debris) with your son or daughter to ensure that he or she understands them.

The Questions

1. What is the meaning of the word *debris*?
   Ⓐ frozen astronaut food
   Ⓑ life on other planets
   Ⓒ scattered pieces of something that has been broken
   Ⓓ a computer malfunction that could put the astronauts in danger

2. What does it mean when an idea is "out of this world"?
   Ⓐ insane
   Ⓑ hard to understand
   Ⓒ fantastic
   Ⓓ scientific

3. Another good title for this article would be:
   Ⓐ "The Space Shuttle"
   Ⓑ "Station in the Sky"
   Ⓒ "An Adventure to the Moon"
   Ⓓ "Blastoff"

4. How fast is the space station moving in orbit?
   Ⓐ 220 miles per hour
   Ⓑ 17,500 miles per hour
   Ⓒ 250 miles per hour
   Ⓓ 2004 miles per hour

We have completed this assignment together.

_____   _____
Child's Signature   Parent's Signature

Week-by-Week Homework for Building Reading Comprehension and Fluency
Scholastic Professional Books

Arctic Disaster!

History Is Filled With People Who Tried—and Failed—to Explore the Arctic

Imagine you're driving a dogsled across dangerous Arctic ice. Cold wind bites at your face. Your fingers are frozen. It's snowing so hard you can barely see the black ears of your dog. The temperature is fifty below zero. You're lost. What do you do?

Modern Arctic and Antarctic explorers can get help in emergencies. They can radio for emergency rescue. Helicopters can swoop in and drop food and supplies. Many early Western explorers went to the Arctic to map it or look for passageways to improve trade. But they were on their own when they became lost or stranded.

The history of polar exploration is full of disasters. One of the first occurred in 1553, when the Englishman Sir Hugh Willoughby and his crew died after their boat was blocked by ice. They didn't have the proper clothing or food to survive the winter.

Today's explorers can choose from high-tech, waterproof fabrics that protect the skin from damaging cold. Special boots protect toes from frostbite. But early Western explorers usually wore leather boots. Sometimes the men's feet got so numb their socks would burn before they felt the heat of a fire!

Food and vitamins were another problem. The freeze-dried foods, nutrition bars, and vitamins of today weren't available. Explorers often suffered from scurvy, a painful disease caused by the lack of vitamin C.

The most famous Arctic disaster was the Franklin expedition. In 1845, Sir John Franklin set out from England with two of the best ships available. When Franklin vanished, at least 40 search parties were sent out. Eventually the remains of the party were found. Some of the men had died from the cold or starvation. Scientists now believe some of the men were poisoned from eating tins of food that weren't prepared properly.

The thick pack ice of the Arctic also caused serious problems for early expeditions. Many explorers had to continue by foot when their boats were crushed by ice. Today, boats in the Arctic are equipped with thick steel hulls to cut through ice. Modern technology also helps ships locate dangerous icebergs. And, of course, since the area has now been mapped, there's far less danger of getting lost.

Robert E. Peary and Matthew Henson, who discovered the North Pole in 1909, were two of the most successful Arctic explorers. Their secret? Unlike most other Western explorers, they spent years living with and learning from the native people, the *Inuit* (IN-yoo-it). Peary and Henson traveled on sleds like the Inuit, wore the same fur boots and parkas, slept in igloos, and learned to hunt and eat the same foods. Their respect for the Inuit way of life helped save their lives.

By Deborah Hopkinson
Reprinted from *Storyworks*, January 2001

75

Dear Parents

Tales of exploration are thrilling to readers young and old—I hope you and your child enjoy reading about the challenges of exploring the Arctic. Your child may encounter several new and difficult words as he or she reads aloud, so you may need to help out with the unfamiliar names and terms.

TIP OF THE WEEK

An important reading skill is the ability to compare and contrast information. This article makes many comparisons between exploration in the past and exploration today. Help your child interpret the article and realize that the author gives information about past and present methods of exploration.

The Questions

Use the information from the text to tell how exploration was different in years past from exploration today. Write sentences on each line to make the comparisons.

Communication Then: _____

_____

Communication Now: _____

_____

Transportation Then: _____

_____

Transportation Now: _____

_____

Clothing Then: _____

_____

Clothing Now: _____

_____

We have completed this assignment together.

_____   _____
Child's Signature   Parent's Signature

Week-by-Week Homework for Building Reading Comprehension and Fluency
Scholastic Professional Books

Zapped!

Getting struck by lightning in real life isn't as much fun as it may seem in science fiction stories. In real life, lightning-strike victims don't get any special powers and quite often they don't live through the experience.

A bolt of lightning is powerful. It can contain enough electricity to flash on all the lights in a medium-sized town. If you were hit by all that energy, bad things would happen:

• Lightning's heat would instantly turn your sweat to steam. That steam could burn your skin and blow your clothes and shoes off.

• Electricity would race through your eyes, ears, nose, and mouth. It would cloud your vision and burst your eardrums.

• The explosive force of lightning could break your bones.

• Your muscles—including your heart—could stop working.

Each year, about 100 people in America die from lightning strikes. Another 400 Americans are struck, but live. That may sound like a lot of people. But almost 261 million people live in the United States. That means only one out of every 522,000 Americans gets struck each year.

Want to be extra sure you're not one of them? Here are some ways to avoid getting zapped:

• Stay inside a solid building during severe thunderstorms. You'll also be safe in a car—as long as it isn't a convertible.

• Avoid pipes, appliances, and talking on the phone during a storm. Lightning can travel through metal pipes and wires.

• If you're forced to stay outside during a thunderstorm, keep away from high places, water, and tall objects. These attract lightning.

• If you can't find shelter, crouch down to make yourself as short as possible.

And always remember this: The best place to experience a lightning strike is in a nice, safe make-believe story.

By Emily Costello
Reprinted from *Storyworks*, February/March 1997

Week-by-Week Homework for Building Reading Comprehension and Fluency
Scholastic Professional Books

Dear Parents

Lightning is beautiful and fascinating—but also very dangerous! As your son or daughter reads this piece aloud to you, he or she will learn more about the power of lightning and how to stay safe.

The Questions

Use your own words to create four bulleted sentences explaining how to stay safe from lightning:

- _____
  _____

- _____
  _____

- _____
  _____

- _____
  _____

We have completed this assignment together.

_____   _____
Child's Signature   Parent's Signature

Week-by-Week Homework for Building Reading Comprehension and Fluency
Scholastic Professional Books

Antarctic Facts

Antarctica is the continent at the South Pole. Antarctica is surrounded by three oceans—the Atlantic, Pacific, and Indian. It is the fifth largest continent and the coldest place on Earth. Because it is below the equator, winter in Antarctica takes place when it is summer in the United States. Metal shatters like glass in the brutal Antarctic winter. Temperatures drop to 120 below zero; a person without the right clothing would freeze solid in just a few minutes. Winds gusting up to 200 miles per hour come screaming down the ice, tearing into piles of snow.

With the exception of a few insects, Antarctica has no animal life on its land. However, penguins, seals, whales, krill, and seabirds thrive in the oceans around the continent. Likewise, few plants besides mosses grow on the ice-covered land of Antarctica.

No people live permanently on this continent, but Antarctica is known for its scientific stations. Many nations, including the U.S., Chile, Norway, Great Britain, and Australia have large research centers where scientists study earthquakes, gravity, oceans, and weather conditions.

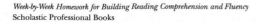

Dear Parents

When students are answering questions about informational articles, it is important that they refer only to the actual article when formulating a response. They should not include background information from a television show or a book they may have read on the same subject unless the question specifically asks them to do so.

TIP OF THE WEEK

Have your child read the passage a second time and use crayons, colored pencils, or highlighters to mark information related to the five categories below; use a different color for each subject. When the time comes to answer the questions, your child should transfer the color-coded words to the proper places. This is a great strategy for organizing information.

The Questions

Write three facts from the story about each of the following topics:

Wildlife in or near Antarctica

1. _____
2. _____
3. _____

Location of Antarctica

1. _____
2. _____
3. _____

Climate of Antarctica

1. _____
2. _____
3. _____

Sciences being studied in Antarctica

1. _____
2. _____
3. _____

List three countries that have scientific stations in Antarctica

1. _____
2. _____
3. _____

We have completed this assignment together.

_____
Child's Signature

_____
Parent's Signature

Week-by-Week Homework for Building Reading Comprehension and Fluency
Scholastic Professional Books

A Crayon Is Born

Nobody Takes Color More Seriously Than the Makers of Crayons

What if you had jungle green hair and atomic tangerine eyes? Hot magenta pants with a blizzard blue shirt?

You can! When you use crayons, you can color yourself any way you want.

Life wasn't always so colorful, though. A hundred years ago, all crayons were black. They were used in factories and shipyards to label crates and lumber. Kids couldn't use them because they were toxic.

Vivid Variety

Then a company called Binney & Smith had an idea. They decided to make Crayola crayons for kids and teachers to use in school. They figured out a formula that was safe, and they also decided to add color. The first box of eight Crayola crayons included black, brown, blue, red, purple, orange, yellow, and green. All of the crayons were labeled by hand. The box cost five cents. The crayons were a huge hit!

Today, many companies make crayons, but Crayola is still the biggest. They take crayons *very* seriously, especially when it comes to color.

For example, Crayola has a team of seven chemists and chemical engineers who do nothing all day but develop new crayon colors. Their laboratory holds the unique, secret formula to every crayon color. They blend different colors to come up with new shades. Once the engineers discover a new color they like, they test it on hundreds of kids and parents to make sure it's really useful. Only then is a crayon ready for the box.

What's in a Name?

Then comes the hard part—figuring out what to name a new color. In 1993, Crayola introduced 16 new colors for its "Big Box" of 96 crayons. More than two million kids and adults wrote in with color name suggestions. Some winners were tickle me pink (bright pink), timber wolf (gray), purple mountains majesty (purple), tropical rainforest (bright green), granny smith apple (light green), and mauvelous (light pink).

Over the years, Crayola has changed some of its color names. In 1962, Crayola changed the name of its crayon color *flesh* to *peach*. They recognized that not everyone's skin is the same color.

Despite all the work Crayola puts into developing new colors, kids' tastes haven't changed much. Around the globe, kids still say that red and blue are their favorite crayon colors.

What are your favorites?

By Lauren Tarshis, Editor, *Storyworks*
Reprinted from *Storyworks*, January 1998

Week-by-Week Homework for Building Reading Comprehension and Fluency
Scholastic Professional Books

Dear Parents

Tonight's homework is about a familiar object—crayons! We often take such common items for granted, never thinking about where they came from or how they're made. I hope you enjoy this entertaining and informative article that fills us in on some fascinating facts about crayons. Don't forget to have your child read it out loud!

The Questions

1. What colors were the first crayons? _____

2. What are the public's two favorite crayon colors? _____

3. Which company makes Crayola crayons? _____

4. How long ago was the "Big Box" of 96 crayons introduced? _____
_____

5. Why were the first Crayola crayons so popular with kids? _____
_____

6. Is it easy to create new crayon colors? Why or why not? _____
_____
_____

We have completed this assignment together.

_____   _____
Child's Signature   Parent's Signature

Week-by-Week Homework for Building Reading Comprehension and Fluency
Scholastic Professional Books

Bananas!!

Banana peels, banana splits, banana breads, bananas on cereal or in milk shakes. America is in love with this fascinating, yummy fruit. But wait. Bananas seem very different from other fruits, like apples and peaches. The seeds inside are very tiny and we eat them, and banana trees don't look like trees at all. That is because they *aren't* trees. The banana is actually a gigantic herb that springs from an underground stem and is considered by scientists to be a form of a berry. This tropical plant is closely related to an exotic, tropical flower, the orchid. What appears to be a trunk is actually a false stem formed by tightly wrapped leaves that grow to a height of nine feet. The flowers that eventually become the bananas we eat grow at the end of a three-foot-long stem. The flowers have huge, pointed purple buds that gradually open to expose the yellow stamens and pistils inside. When the plant is full of 20 to 30 bananas, the whole thing is called a "hand" and is picked while all of the bananas are still green.

Bananas have a long tradition in American history. They were introduced to the United States in 1876 at the Philadelphia Centennial Exhibition (a year-long celebration commemorating America's 100th birthday). Each banana was wrapped in foil and sold for 10 cents—about the same cost as a banana today! The average American eats about 10 pounds of bananas a year, but the average European eats almost 22 pounds!

Want to stay young? Bananas are an excellent source of potassium, which is thought to retard the aging process. Want a snack before a fast game? They also contain lots of easily digested carbohydrates for quick energy. Want to stay healthy? Bananas have large amounts of Vitamins A and C. Want to eat healthy foods but stay thin? Bananas are low in protein and fat and are an excellent between-meal snack. A medium-sized banana has only about 125 to 130 calories. Have a tummy ache? Bananas are one of the most easily digested and nutritious foods.

And how else do we like our bananas? In muffins, cakes, suspended in jello? Or dipped in chocolate and frozen on a stick? Layered on bread with peanut butter? These are all great, but no, the favorite way to eat a banana is just to eat it! It is perfectly packaged in a throwaway, recyclable container (its peel), can be carried anywhere, and doesn't need refrigeration. Don't you want to eat one of these delicious yellow *berries* right now?

By Mary Rose

83

Dear Parents

As your child reads this article aloud, listen for how the author presents the positive characteristics of this favorite fruit, the banana. Help your child see that an author's purpose in writing about a subject affects how he or she presents the information. This is a good first step toward encouraging kids to critically view television commercials and magazine ads.

The Questions

1. What two things are in the article just to make the banana sound interesting to you, the reader?

1. _____

2. _____

2. This article was written to persuade you to eat a banana. Persuasive writing must point out how certain actions will benefit you, the reader. How can your life be better if you eat a banana?

1. _____

2. _____

3. _____

We have completed this assignment together.

_____   _____
Child's Signature   Parent's Signature

Week-by-Week Homework for Building Reading Comprehension and Fluency
Scholastic Professional Books

Chapter 6

Popular Culture

Passages	Skill Focus	Standard
Under the Big Top	✳ Interpreting figurative language	✳ Understands and interprets figurative language
The History of a Toy	✳ Identifying cause and effect	✳ Recognizes cause-and-effect relationships
Ozified!	✳ Identifying author's purpose	✳ Identifies author's purpose ✳ Identifies supporting details
Want Fries With That?	✳ Recognizing appositives	✳ Uses text features to enhance comprehension

Kids will love reading about the circus, the yo-yo, *The Wizard of Oz*, and McDonald's! Why not capitalize on kids' interest in popular culture to help them become better and more critical readers. These selections do just that.

Under the Big Top

Skill focus: Interpreting Figurative Language

The English language is full of colorful words and phrases that can enrich speech and writing. "Under the Big Top" presents some figurative language we use every day that originated with the circus. Since children often have a difficult time interpreting figurative language, this is a great forum for introducing the idea and sparking kids' curiosity about language. Encourage your students to be on the lookout for new and different words and phrases and to investigate their origins—and then use them in their writing! Check out *The Scholastic Dictionary of Idioms, Phrases, Sayings, and Expressions* by Marvin Terban (Scholastic Inc., 1996) for a short history of other famous and common sayings.

The History of a Toy

Skill focus: Identifying Cause and Effect

Many states no longer test students' understanding of cause and effect on their curriculum tests, but the concept is almost universally listed under state reading standards. To help children understand cause and effect, start by working backwards. Look at the effect first and decide what could have caused this to happen. Have students state the effect followed by the word *because*, and then have them say or write the cause of the event. For example: We will not go out to the playground (effect) because of the rain (cause). We will not have math today (an effect) because of the assembly. (The assembly is the cause of the cancellation of math class.)

Ozified!

Skill focus: Identifying Author's Purpose

This piece fills readers in on a piece of American culture—the film version of *The Wonderful Wizard of Oz*. The author provides lots of facts and figures to educate her readers about the film's history, something our students probably don't know about! The author's purpose—to inform—is clear, and there are plenty of examples students can draw on to support that judgment, a skill the new performance assessments require for author's purpose questions.

Follow-up: One way to help children answer questions such as number four from the homework—"Why does the author include the fact that one billion people have seen this movie?"—is to ask them how the article would affect them differently if the author had omitted that piece of information. Would they have still felt the same way about the movie or about this article? Would they have felt that they learned something new? By looking at the article with that fact omitted, students can see the impact specific information can have.

Want Fries With That?

Skill focus: Recognizing Appositives

This fun article on one of America's favorite foods is a great way to teach about appositives. Recognizing that the definition of a word or phrase is included right there in the sentence is an invaluable skill—for test takers, students, and readers alike. Be sure to point out that the word before the phrase set off by commas (the appositive) is the word being defined. As I tell my students, appositives are test questions waiting to happen!

Under the Big Top

Have you ever heard the phrase *Come rain or shine?* How about the word *jumbo* or *big top?* All of these phrases have become part of the English language because of one man and his one very big idea.

Phineas Taylor Barnum is the man behind these familiar phrases. He created "The Greatest Show on Earth," The Ringling Brothers and Barnum and Bailey Circus. As the original circus traveled around the country in the late 1800s, Americans heard these words and phrases and began to use them. Soon everyone forgot that they ever had a connection with the circus.

One time during a circus performance, a man who wanted to run for an elective office stood up and threw his hat into the circus ring just to get everyone's attention. The whole show stopped while he announced his name and said that he wanted to be elected. Even today when someone decides to run for an elective office, we say that they will "throw their hat into the ring."

The traveling circus would come to a town and stay for a few days or a week and perform several shows. When it was time to load up all of the tents, animals, peformers and equipment, the circus people would say it was time to "get the show on the road" and head for the next town. We still use this phrase as a way to indicate that it is time to get started on something.

If you have ever been to an arena or stadium, it is obvious to you that some seats are more expensive than others because they give you a better view of the show. These expensive seats were originally called the "grand stands," and people wanted to sit there to show off that they were important. We still say that people who are showing off are "grandstanding."

The largest circus tents were called the "big top." The one tent would cover about three acres. That's probably bigger than your school playground! We still talk about things "under the big top" when we mean something really large. And speaking of large, Mr. Barnum introduced the word *jumbo* to mean something really huge. This time it was a white elephant that he named Jumbo. Today a "white elephant" is something that no one really wants in their home and "jumbo" still means oversized.

One hundred years ago, shows would be canceled because of bad weather, but the Barnum circus went on "come rain or shine." P. T. Barnum's was the first business to use this as an advertising phrase—and we still use it today.

Now you know the origin of some of our most common phrases. But the one that P. T. Barnum is most famous for is, "There's a sucker born every minute." See if you can figure out what this phrase means; if not, ask an adult.

Adapted from "Prince of Humbugs" from *Explore* magazine by Mary Rose

Week-by-Week Homework for Building Reading Comprehension and Fluency
Scholastic Professional Books

Dear Parents

American English is a rich language, full of colorful words and phrases. This article describes P. T. Barnum's circus—an American tradition—and discusses some of the language from the circus that we still use today. Enjoy!

The Questions

Write an original sentence (with a grown-up's help!) in which you can use each of the following phrases:

1. Come rain or come shine: _____

_____

2. Under the big top: _____

_____

3. Grandstanding: _____

_____

4. Jumbo: _____

_____

5. Get the show on the road: _____

_____

We have completed this assignment together.

_____   _____
Child's Signature   Parent's Signature

Week-by-Week Homework for Building Reading Comprehension and Fluency
Scholastic Professional Books

The History of a Toy

Look in your toy box and try to guess which toys are modern and which have been played with by children throughout history. Which toy do you think has the most history and can be traced back the furthest in time? How about the yo-yo? Surprised? The yo-yo is believed to have originated in China about 2,500 years ago. Explorers have even found drawings of yo-yos on ancient Egyptian temples. Back then they were not plastic, of course, but were made of wood or clay and were just called "discs."

Today we think of a yo-yo as being a child's toy, but in the late 1700s King Louis XVII played with a toy "emigrette"—a yo-yo made of glass and ivory. In the opera *The Marriage of Figaro*, the nervous Figaro shows he is upset by constantly playing with an emigrette. Even the soldiers of Napoleon's army played with yo-yos to calm their nerves before going out to do battle. In 1791 the emigrette became known as the "Prince of Wales Toy," and was still played with mostly by adults.

In 1866 the yo-yo finally made it to the United States when two men from Ohio received a patent for what they called the "bandalore," a yo-yo with a weighted rim.

The yo-yo was also known as the Filipino Toy. In 1920 Pedro Flores brought the first Filipino yo-yo to the United States and began a company in California. In 1928 Donald F. Duncan Sr. saw this toy and liked the idea so much that he bought the whole company from Flores and renamed the toy the "yo-yo." The Duncan Company moved to Luck, Wisconsin, which became known as the yo-yo capital of the world and was producing 3,600 wooden yo-yos per hour. Duncan decided to promote the yo-yo to children by teaching them how to use it and how to do tricks with it. He hired people to go all over the United States holding contests and demonstrating tricks. The yo-yo became wildly popular. By 1962 the Duncan Company had sold 45 million yo-yos and the country had only 40 million kids! It seemed that there was a yo-yo on every corner and in every home in the USA! Indeed, many adults were *still* playing with yo-yos!

After a few years, the word *yo-yo* became so popular that the Duncan Company could no longer claim the name for itself. When other companies were able to use the name yo-yo, the Duncan Company lost so much business that it filed for bankruptcy and closed in 1965. Today, the Flambeau Plastic Company still makes and sells eleven different models of the popular Duncan yo-yo. One new kind even has a "brain," so that it will return to the holder's hand if it begins to spin too slowly.

So look into your toy box again and this time pull out a yo-yo. See if you can get it to "sleep" or if you can remember how to "rock the cradle" or "walk the dog." Then try to imagine children (and adults) in far off lands and times playing with the same basic toy that you are holding.

By Mary Rose

Week-by-Week Homework for Building Reading Comprehension and Fluency
Scholastic Professional Books

Dear Parents

I hope you and your child will both learn something new in this article about a favorite children's toy, the yo-yo. There are several difficult words in here— including bankruptcy and emigrette. Please help your child to determine what these unfamiliar words might mean by looking at how they are used in the sentences. Remember to have your child read the entire passage out loud to you.

TIP OF THE WEEK

Determining cause and effect is challenging for young students. Just like they don't seem to realize that having gum in class (cause) will get you in trouble with the teacher (effect), they also fail to recognize it in their reading material. You can help your child to understand these concepts by using the terms *cause* and *effect* in conversations: "If you get your homework done quickly (cause), you will have time to watch television (effect). If you save your money (cause), you will have enough to buy a new catcher's mitt (effect)."

The Questions

1. At first, only adults played with the yo-yo. What **effect** did this have on the adults?

   _____

2. What was the **cause** of the problem for the Duncan Company in 1965? _____

   _____

3. What was the **effect** on the company? _____

   _____

4. What will **cause** a yo-yo with a brain to return to the holder's hand? _____

   _____

5. What is the **effect** of having a yo-yo with a brain? _____

   _____

We have completed this assignment together.

_____   _____
Child's Signature   Parent's Signature

Week-by-Week Homework for Building Reading Comprehension and Fluency
Scholastic Professional Books

Ozified!

"Ozified" is the term that MGM studios used to describe the entire United States in 1939 when the movie *The Wizard of Oz* first came out. There was a special radio broadcast about the movie and most newspapers featured Oz stories to get people interested in the film. It was the very first time that a movie release was accompanied by the sales of books, toys, dolls, games, soaps, Valentines, and dresses! The sales of these items were expected to hype the movie and entice people to go see it. And the hype worked. *The Wizard of Oz* was wildly successful. Ten thousand people gathered just to greet the film's stars and production staff on opening night. Thousands more from California to New York paid to see it. But the movie just broke even, meaning that it made only enough money to cover what it cost to make it.

The Wizard of Oz was considered a very expensive movie to make. It cost more than three million dollars—an astounding amount of money in 1939! Even though the movie was wildly popular, it didn't even make back the three million until it finally started being shown on television starting in 1956. From 1956 to 1988 it was shown every year and finally grossed about twenty million dollars. It was also re-released in movie theaters and made another five million there. And we are still "Ozified!" as the lure of this wonderful film continues to pull in home-video viewers. But there is a long story behind the path to the video.

The Wizard of Oz as we know it was not the first production of this wonderful story, written by L. Frank Baum in 1896. In 1902 it was performed as a play on Broadway in New York City. Then it was made into a silent movie in 1908, 1910, 1914, and 1925. Imagine having to read the words to know that the Scarecrow needed a brain and that Dorothy was trying to get back to Kansas!

When the 1939 version of *The Wizard of Oz* was first shown in New York, Judy Garland would actually appear on the stage with Mickey Rooney for a 30-minute song and dance between showings of the film. The teenage couple performed their act five times during the week and several times a day on weekends!

Ozified? Yes. There are Oz references everywhere in our language and culture. We often speak of "following the yellow-brick road" or a person with "straw for brains." It is not uncommon for someone to say "You're not in Kansas anymore, Dorothy," when a person is encountering a new situation.

Items from the movie are also very popular. In 1988 a bidder paid $168,000 for Dorothy's ruby red slippers. It was the most money anyone had ever paid for a piece of movie memorabilia. *The Wizard of Oz* has been seen by more people than any other entertainment in the history of the world. Its audience now tops over one billion people. Ozified, indeed!

By Mary Rose

Week-by-Week Homework for Building Reading Comprehension and Fluency
Scholastic Professional Books

Dear Parents

"The Wizard of Oz" is a classic movie that has become part of American culture. This article provides some background on the film, but if your child has not seen the movie, he or she may need extra help with the assignment.

TIP OF THE WEEK

Identifying an author's purpose is an important reading skill. Often, the purpose is to persuade, inform, or entertain the reader. You can help your child remember these purposes with the acronym **PIE**, an effective mnemonic device. But today's tests ask students to discuss an author's purpose in paragraph form, meaning they must provide support for their answer by including examples from the text.

The Questions

1. Why did the author explain the item "Ozified" in the opening paragraphs of the article?

   _____

   _____

2. Why does the author include the fact that one billion people have seen this movie?

   _____

   _____

3. What was the author's purpose for writing this article? Support your answers with examples from the text. _____

   _____

   _____

   _____

   _____

   _____

We have completed this assignment together.

_____   _____
Child's Signature   Parent's Signature

Want Fries With That?

Don't even bother to ask—the answer is, yes, we do want fries with that. The average American annually eats about 30 pounds of frozen fries, or about four servings of fries a week. And yet, what do we really know about these little golden sticks of greasy goodness. Where did they come from, and how did they get to be America's No. 1 fast-food item?

Some say it was World War I that made fries famous in the United States. The Belgians say it was while American **GIs**, or soldiers, were stationed in Belgium during World War I, that they first got a taste of deep fried potato sticks. But because of poor geography skills, or because many Belgians spoke French, the GIs assumed they were in French territory. So when they returned to the United States, they spoke of the wonderful French fries "over there."

There is a science involved in making perfect fries. In the United States, the primary potatoes used for making fries are russets. The type of potato is important because its water and sugar contents will affect the outcome at the time of frying. McDonald's is the largest purchaser of potatoes in the United States. McDonald's fries are considered the **benchmark**, the fries all other fast-food outlets try to copy. Millions of dollars and innumerable hours of research went into perfecting the process of cooking, freezing, and cooking again the fries that made McDonald's famous.

Here's how McDonald's makes its fries. The potatoes are aged until they achieve the right amount of water content and the proper amount of sugar has converted to starch. Then they are washed and put through a steam process that removes the peel. Then the potatoes are **frenched**, a term that means to cut vegetables into strips, to about a quarter-inch square. Then they are **blanched**, a process in which food is placed into boiling water for a brief period and then plunged into icy water to arrest the cooking. Then they are dried and **par-fried**, which means they are partially cooked in boiling oil.

After par-frying, the fries are **flash-frozen**, meaning that they are frozen very quickly at extremely low temperatures, packaged and shipped to McDonald's around the country at the rate of about 2 million pounds a day!

It's at your neighborhood McDonald's of course, that the final frying process takes place, in a special computerized deep-fryer that monitors the temperature of the oil and signals when the fries have been cooked to a color as perfect as the Golden Arches. Finally, the fries are salted and served to you piping hot.

Want fries with that? Of course we do!

Originally titled "A Super-Sized Obsession"
by Scott Joseph in the Orlando Sentinel, August 24, 2001.

Week-by-Week Homework for Building Reading Comprehension and Fluency
Scholastic Professional Books

Dear Parents

Please listen to your child read this article about McDonald's french fries. Perhaps both of you can learn something new about one of America's favorite foods!

The Questions

Use your own words to write a definition of each of the words below.
The definition should apply to how the word is used in this article only.
Sample: 30 pounds of frozen fries <u>This is the amount of fries the average American eats in a year.</u>

1. GIs _____

_____

2. benchmark _____

_____

3. frenched _____

_____

4. blanched _____

_____

5. flash-frozen _____

_____

We have completed this assignment together.

_____   _____
Child's Signature   Parent's Signature

Week-by-Week Homework for Building Reading Comprehension and Fluency
Scholastic Professional Books

Answers

Answers to Questions on Page 17
1. Forty million people lived in North and South America when Columbus arrived.
2. A potato is similar to manioc.
3. A game of batey would look like a soccer match.
4. The Arawaks made a canoe by lighting fires in a log and scooping out the ashes with stone tools.

Answers to Questions on Page 19
1. Pilgrim children had to stand up to eat. We get to sit down. 2. Pilgrim children were not allowed to talk. We talk all of the time. 3. Pilgrim children had to walk everywhere they went. We get to ride in cars. 4. Pilgrim children had few toys; we have many.

Answers to Questions on Page 21
1. A macaroni is a men's hairstyle. The men wore their hair long and tied up in a bun on top of their heads.
2. A doodle was another word for a fool.
3. A Yankee was an uneducated person who did not understand proper society.
4. The American soldiers sang the song because they thought it would irritate the British.

Answers to Questions on Page 23
1. donate: to give as a gift without receiving money in return. 2. stupendous: amazing, astonishing. 3. appointed: designated day, the established or settled day. 4. diameter: straight line passing through the center of a circle. 5. hoisted: to be lifted with a mechanical device.

Answers to Questions on Page 25
1. "We spread our wings as a new nations" means that our country was beginning to act like a real country. It wanted to "grow up" and expand and become larger. 2. "We hit a big snag" means that something has gone wrong with the plan. Descriptive words: stormed, gobbled, stinging eyes

Answers to Questions on Page 27
Sample student responses: 1. Life was dangerous because the children had to use a gun to go hunting for food and girls went into the forest to gather berries. 2. Life was exciting because there were Indians to meet and t trade with. 3. Life was hard because of the primitive lifestyle; many had to live in a tent or a shelter of pine boughs and everyone had to do a lot of work.

Answers to Questions on Page 33
1. nugget: stone, rock 2. exhausted: tired, pooped 3. speared: puncture, stabbed 4. dread: dismay, panic, worry, fret 5. grieved: mourn, sadden, cry, weep.

Answers to Questions on Page 35
1. There is indentation for a new paragraph. 2. Quotation marks appear. 3. The word "said," or other speaking word shows up.

Answers to Questions on Page 37
Words to describe Tell: brave, caring, strong, talented, stubborn, determined.
Words to describe Gessler: mean, demanding, overpowering, cruel, devious.
Sentences: I think William Tell was strong because he was able to pull back the bow and no other man in Switzerland could do that. I think William Tell was brave because he took the chance of killing his son when he was forced to shoot the arrow. I think Gessler was mean because he put a child in prison. I think Gessler was demanding because he wanted everyone to bow down to his hat.

Answers to Questions on Page 39
1. The rattlesnake tricked the rabbit by making him think that he would not harm him if the rabbit would help out. The rattlesnake tricked the rabbit by offering him a "reward" that was not really a reward at all. 2. The coyote tricked the rattlesnake by having him show how the rabbit found him. The coyote tricked the rattlesnake by putting him back where he started out in the story, with no one to help him. 3. The moral of the story is not to trust dishonest and untrustworthy people, no matter what they promise. The moral of the story is to be grateful when someone helps you out. 4. The author's purpose was to entertain the reader.

Answers to Questions on Page 42
1. Plumb: clear, as in clear over the house. 2. Rations: food and ingredients with which to cook a meal. 3. Thaw: snow and ice are melting. 4. Trimmin': trimming, cutting the smaller branches off of the tree. 5. See-sawin': sliding back and forth up and down the valley. 6. Trough: the area in the valley between the two mountains.

Answers to Questions on Page 45
The repetitive phrases are "Including the crown which the Queen sometimes liked to wear to sleep"; reference to "Someone who has Everything"; and "three feet wide and six feet long."
The repetitive actions occur whenever the king and apprentice are trying to communicate. The King calls the Prime Minister, who calls the Chief Carpenter, who calls the apprentice. This process is reversed when the apprentice needs to communicate. Other repeated actions occur when the King repeatedly tells the Queen to put on her new pajamas.

Answers to Questions on Page 50
Students can cite any 10 facts from the article.

Answers to Questions on Page 52
1. Tazio was born in Italy. Tazio was born in 1892. Tazio raced motorcycles before he raced cars. Tazio raced a motorcycle with two broken legs. 2. Tazio didn't mind pain. Tazio was very clever. Tazio was a legend in the racing world. Tazio was a talented and brave driver. Everyone thought Tazio was a legend. 3. The author's purpose is to inform the audience of a legendary figure in auto racing.

Answers to Questions on Page 54
1. Dr. Kountz taught other doctors how best to transport organs from patient to patient so they could be transplanted. 2. He studied biochemistry at the University of Arkansas in Fayetteville. He established a kidney transplant and research center. He performed an operation live on the *Today* show.

Answers to Questions on Page 56
1. The word in parentheses is "serious," which defines "dramatic." 2. The sentence following "stand-up comedian," explains what it is. 3. The words after the first dash are "no tricks, no songs." These words explain the previous phrase, "nothing but talk." The second words following the dash are "making people laugh." They explain what Cosby enjoyed most. The words in italics are the names of television shows or books.

Answers to Questions on Page 61
Verbs: scream, shout, call, signaling, yell, tell, howl, naming, wail, counting, shriek.
Samples of verbs the poet could have used: cry, rip, cover, break, tear, freeze, drip.
Bonus: The second line of each stanza becomes the first line of the following stanza.

Answers to Questions on Page 64
1. The Mudville baseball team was losing 2 to 4. 2. Flynn and Blake both made it to base, so Casey was up next. 3. The first two balls went by as strikes. 4. Casey struck out.

Answers to Questions on Page 66
1. Can be any set of rhyming words at the end of any set of lines. Example: mumps, bumps; rows, clothes. 2. Both of these poems happen at home; both poems concern school; both students end up realizing that it is Saturday; both children really didn't want to go to school. 3. One poem is just a dream about school; the other is not a dream; One child is pretending to be sick so he can miss school; the other is just having a nightmare about going to school. One has another person talking in it; the other is all one person. One is long and the other is short.

Answers to Questions on Page 69
1. The lamb followed Mary everywhere because she had always taken care of it. 2. The other children laughed at the lamb. 3. It was not a good idea to take the lamb to school because the teacher didn't like it and the children laughed at Mary. 4. Short paragraph should include three to five sentences about a pet.

Answers to Questions on Page 74
1. C 2. C 3. B 4. B

Answers to Questions on Page 76
Communication: Then explorers would be lost and no one could find them. Now we have radios for emergency use. Then explorers would be lost because there were no maps. Now we have better maps so they don't get lost. Transportation: Then they had to depend on their boats to get them back home. Now we have helicopters to help get people out. Then they had wooden boats. Now we have boats with steel hulls that can break through the ice. Clothing: Then they wore leather boots and animal parkas. Now we have special high-tech waterproof fabrics and special boots to save us from frostbite. Food: Then they sometimes ate poison food and lacked vitamins and minerals. Today they have freeze-dried foods and vitamins.

Answers to Questions on Page 78
You can be safe in a lightning storm if you:
stay in a car that is not a convertible; stay in a safe building; stay away from the stove and the refrigerator; don't talk on the telephone; stay away from water such as lakes; lay on the ground; stay away from trees.

Answers to Questions on Page 80
Wildlife: There's none on land except insects. Penguins, seals, whales, krill, and sea birds live in the oceans.
Location: It's surrounded by three oceans: the Atlantic, the Pacific, and the Indian Ocean. It's below the equator. It's at the South Pole.
Climate: It's brutal. The temperature can drop to 120 below zero. Winds blow at up to 200 miles an hour. There's lots of snow and ice.
Sciences: Earthquakes, gravity, oceans, and weather conditions are all studied.
Countries: USA, Chile, Norway, Great Britain, Australia all have stations there.

Answers to Questions on Page 82
1. black; 2. red and blue; 3. Binney and Smith; 4. Subtract 1996 from current year; 5. The first Crayola crayons were popular because kids could use them and they were colorful; 6. It is not easy to create new crayon colors. Engineers try out lots of colors and test them out on kids. Then they have to name the new colors.

Answers to Questions on Page 84
1. The banana is actually a berry and the banana tree is not a tree. The author gives a little bit of history about the banana and tells us that it still doesn't cost very much to eat. 2. If you eat bananas, you will stay young, have lots of energy, not be fat, get extra vitamins, be eating a healthy food, will not be hungry, won't get an upset tummy.

Answers to Questions on Page 88
1. "We will have this spelling test come rain or come shine." 2. "Our soccer team is under the big top now." 3. "He was just grandstanding when he said he bowled a perfect game." 4. "I want the jumbo order of fries." 5. "Mom yelled at us kids to hurry up and get the show on the road."

Answers to Questions on Page 90
1. The yo-yo had a calming effect on the adults who played with it. 2. The cause of the problem for the Duncan Company in 1965 is that other companies could now use the word yo-yo in selling their products. 3. The effect was that the Duncan Company filed for bankruptcy. 4. The yo-yo with a brain will return to the hand of the holder if it spins too slowly. 5. The effect is that the player rarely has to pause and rewind a stopped toy.

Answers to Questions on Page 92
1. The author explained "Ozified" in the opening paragraph because it was the title of the article and so that children could relate to the hype that movies offer to us today. 2. The author wants you to know that this is a really popular movie. By including the actual figure, it is more effective than just saying that lots of people watched it. 3. This article was written to inform.

Answers to Questions on Page 94
1. GIs: These letters refer to men in service such as the army. 2. benchmark: a high level of achievement by which others are judged. In this case McDonald's fries are considered the best and everyone else is trying to get theirs to be as good. 3. frenched: a style of cutting vegetables into long thin strips. 4. blanched: to plunge a vegetable into boiling water and then into icy water. 5. flash frozen: frozen quickly at a low temperature.